PRAISE FOR *MAKING FRIENDS*
'Simple, lucid advice on how to accept
Matt Haig, Sunday Times Bestselli

'Sarah's advice is very sage. Deeply personal, yet eminently practical, this accessible and engaging book should prove extremely helpful to anyone trying to cope with anxiety.'
Dr Ian Williams, GP and author

'A self-help book packed with tips, exercises, and insights to ease worry and panic, this reads like chatting with an old friend; one with wit, wisdom and experience. Perfect for anyone suffering from this difficult disorder.'
The Book Doctor, Brighton and Hove Independent

PRAISE FOR *THE 5:2 DIET BOOK:*
'The go-to 5:2 bible... Kate's inspiring tone, motivational tips and simple menu ideas make this book a convert's best bud.'
Women's Fitness

PRAISE FOR SARAH RAYNER:
'Brilliant... Warm and approachable.' **Essentials**
'Carefully crafted and empathetic.' **Sunday Times**
'A sympathetic insight into the causes and effects of mental ill-health as it affects ordinary people. Powerful.' **My Weekly**
'Explores an emotive subject with great sensitivity.'
Sunday Express

PRAISE FOR KATE HARRISON:
'Warm and witty.' **The Evening Telegraph**
'Poignant and funny.' **She**
'A very readable page-turner... Interesting and thought-provoking.' **Book Trust**

Making Friends: A series of warm, supportive guides to help you on life's journey

Sarah Rayner

Making Friends with Anxiety:

A warm, supportive little book to help ease worry and panic

More Making Friends with Anxiety:

A little book of creative activities to help reduce stress and worries

Sarah Rayner and Dr Patrick Fitzgerald

Making Friends with the Menopause:

A clear and comforting guide to support you as your body changes

Making Peace with the End of Life:

A warm, supportive guide to separating and starting anew

Sarah Rayner and Tracey Sainsbury

Making Friends with your Fertility:

A clear and comforting guide to reproductive health

Sarah Rayner and Pia Pasternack

Making Peace with Divorce:

A warm and wise companion to recovery

By Sarah Rayner and Jules Miller

Making Friends with Anxiety: A Calming Colouring Book

Non-fiction by Kate Harrison:

The 5:2 Diet Book

The Ultimate 5:2 Recipe Book

5:2 Your Life

5:2 Good Food Kitchen

5:2 Veggie & Vegan

SARAH RAYNER
KATE HARRISON
DR PATRICK FITZGERALD

Making Peace with Depression

Illustrated by Sarah Rayner

First published November 2016
This edition November 2017

This edition first published in 2017 by Creative Pumpkin Publishing, an imprint of The Creative Pumpkin Ltd., 5 Howard Terrace, Brighton, East Sussex, BN1 3TR. **www.creativepumpkinpublishing.com**

Creative Pumpkin
Publishing

www.sarah-rayner.com
www.kate-harrison.com

Publisher's Note:

Making Peace with Depression provides information on a wide range of health and medical matters, but is not intended as a substitute for professional diagnosis. Any person with a condition or symptoms requiring medical attention should consult a fully qualified practitioner or therapist. While the advice and information in the book are believed to be accurate and true at the time of going to press, the authors cannot accept any legal responsibility or liability for any errors or omissions that may have been made, nor for any inaccuracies nor for any loss, harm or injury that comes from following instructions of advice in this book.

Hello and welcome

Maybe you've spent a chunk of the day locked in the loo at work, crying. Maybe you're so drained by looking after your kids or elderly relatives that the smallest task seems overwhelming. Maybe you feel swamped by professional responsibilities, or you're in bed and just can't get up. Or maybe you feel that you're going under, and can't pinpoint why. Whatever has led you to this book, if you're in a head space like this, it's awful. I know because I've been there.

People may tell you to 'pull yourself together', or not believe there is anything wrong with you. Whilst they may mean well, neither is going to help. I know that if you *could* pull yourself together, you would, and I *do* understand what the matter is: it's likely that you are suffering from extremely low mood, or a very bad and prolonged case of the blues. Often it's called depression.

Depression is not a black and white issue

Lots of people feel uncomfortable around the word 'depression', and they certainly don't like to think they may be depressed. But before you say 'Pah! That's not me', and stop reading, hear me out. I believe depression isn't a 'you-either-have-it-or-you-don't' scenario – our moods lie on more of a spectrum than that. Nor am I labelling you; I'm suggesting that *if* the opening sentences of this book sound similar to how you're feeling, chances are that you are currently closer to the very low mood or depressed end of the spectrum than the happy and optimistic end. Moreover, it's *your* spectrum that matters, not anyone else's. You may never be particularly bouncy or upbeat, and that's fine – we can't all be live wires, and a world without quiet, thoughtful people would be a poorer place. It's **feeling a long way from *your* normal self that is key, as depression can distort our ability to think clearly about everything and everyone including ourselves,** leaving us sensing that we've lost part of ourselves along the way.

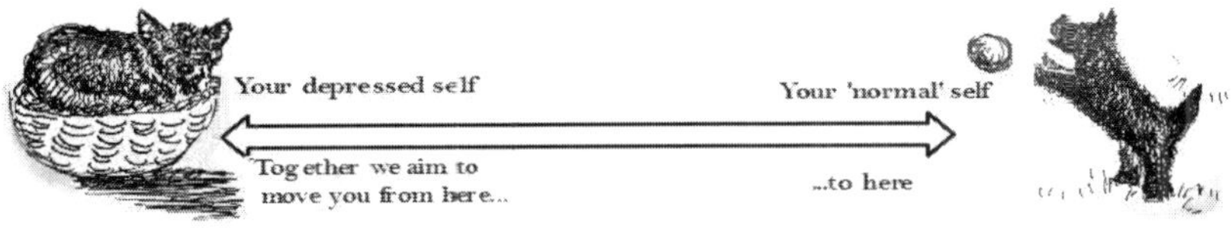

If you're suffering from depression right now I appreciate it might not seem like it, but **the fact that depression isn't a black and white issue is good news in terms of your recovery**. To turn black into white or vice versa is an impossibility, but because depression is not something you have or don't have in an either/or fashion, it *is* possible to slide along the spectrum so your mood gradually evolves from extremely low to less low to OK, and hopefully, eventually, to 'normal', however that is for you individually. For these reasons I'm not going to claim this book can 'cure' depression; depression isn't a viral illness like measles or mumps. Nor shall I talk of 'beating' depression; depression isn't a competition that we either win or lose.

Instead **this book aims to help you understand depression more fully, make you more aware of your moods and what triggers you, and explore the tools that may help ease it over time**. This will be a gentle and supportive process with no pummelling or beating of the mind involved. It is also why this book is called *Making Peace with Depression*, however strange that may seem in the context of an agonizing mental experience. Together we'll explore how **hating depression, wishing it would go away or seeing it as your enemy can maintain and even exacerbate very low mood, whereas compassionate acceptance of our feelings and ourselves can help release us**. Stick with these tools and maintain self-awareness, and gradually your depression should ease. Furthermore, these tools can help you manage your moods better in the future.

About me, Sarah Rayner

At this point you might ask, 'So what makes *you* an authority on depression?' and I admit that I'm not a doctor or therapist. I'm just a ordinary person (whatever 'ordinary' is), who has experienced several depressive episodes. The worst was when I was thirty; I suffered what some call a breakdown. I'd had a major operation which affected my hormones, then went on and off antidepressants too fast. The chemical changes were too much for my brain and I lost it for a few weeks. I knew who I was (just) and I didn't hallucinate, but pretty much everything else walloped me — paranoia, fear of dying, dreadful insomnia and overwhelming panic. It felt like a living hell.

Before then I'd been OK. I'd had my heart broken by a boyfriend or three and may have broken a couple of hearts myself. I'd been to university and had a ball, and although I'd had glandular fever which laid me physically and mentally low for months in my mid-twenties, I'd experienced nothing — *nothing* — like full-on depression. At the time it felt an eternity, and I don't say that lightly. Because our minds seem the seat of our sense of self (though actually they're inextricably linked to our bodies, as I'll come on to later), when our thoughts disintegrate, it can seem as if our very personalities have gone. And because it had not happened to me before, I'd no idea — no 'proof' — I would come out the other side. I thought I would be hospitalized and spend the rest of my days in an institution. I was wrong.

This is the first and most pressing thing I want to tell you because at my worst it's what I desperately needed to hear: **YOU ARE NOT GOING TO FEEL THIS WAY FOREVER**. However bad you feel — whether you're crying every day, believe you're going mad, are drawn to self-harm, whatever — these feelings *will* pass.

Please trust me here. You *will* get better. It won't necessarily happen that fast, and you'll have to be patient, which I know is horribly hard when you're in such a painful place, but **there is a way through**. And whilst I can't promise you'll never feel wobbly again, for me the first time it happened was the scariest because I didn't know I would resurface. In fact, I felt much happier within months, and now it's just one of the many experiences I've had in my life, alongside getting a degree, being dumped, writing novels and meeting my husband, though not one I recall with pleasure. You too can come to see depression as a very dark period in the full colour sweep of your life, once you have some distance from it. But first we have to move through it, and that's what this book aims to help with.

About this book

Let me kick off by introducing my co-authors.

Kate Harrison is the author of four non-fiction books about health and diet, as well as twelve novels. She worked as an investigative journalist and BBC correspondent and developed a broad knowledge of diet and nutrition when she embarked on intermittent fasting, which led her to writing the bestseller, *The 5:2 Diet Book* — it's been translated into 15 languages. Kate has also experienced episodes of depression since her teens, and has applied her journalistic curiosity to finding practical and evidence-based strategies to deal with the condition. She says: 'Depression isn't something anyone welcomes, but it's taught me a lot about myself and living a better life. I'm really excited to share what I've learned.' So that it's clear when Kate is writing, you'll find her contributions are in a different typeface, like this.

Kate and I are also friends who support one another just as we hope this book will support you. Neither of us want this book to mislead you on any of the clinical aspects of depression or the medications that you may be prescribed, however, yet neither of us is a medical expert. Luckily, we know a man who is.

Patrick Fitzgerald currently works as a GP in a small town in Cheshire. 'I consult patients with mental health concerns and depression on a daily basis in my work as a doctor,' says Patrick. 'So I'm keen to make clear and concise information widely available.' You'll find his contributions in grey, like this.

Investing in your own mental health

If you're feeling very desperate, you may be doubtful that simply reading a book on depression can improve things. Or if you're not so bad, you might reason that everyone gets upset, or that lying awake night after night churning over your problems isn't that big a deal. Yet surely it's worth investing *some* time in your own wellbeing? This book can be read in a few hours – not a huge outlay of time when weighed against months or possibly years of suffering. This equation is true no matter what form your depression takes – in fact it's more important if you're close to rock bottom to focus on your needs as your mental health could benefit from urgent attention. If you're at this point now, we suggest you head straight to Chapter 7.

Here's how we aim to make a difference with this book:

1. Understanding what is happening can help – a lot. Whilst depression manifests itself differently in all of us, Kate and I have had several bouts between us, and over the years have both become experts on depression – our *own* depression. But whilst we've both drawn on our experiences in what follows, this book is *not* a memoir of either of us. Ultimately **you are the focus**, not us, and we hope to help you gain more understanding of yourself.

2. This book is written with honesty. It doesn't make false promises. We do not believe in miracles and we feel that anyone who suggests they can get rid of your low mood forever is talking claptrap. No one is 100% happy all the time. But **you can be happier than you are right now.**

3. It aims to show you why low mood isn't a bad thing *per se*. Much as you might want to be rid of depression right now, in some ways it can actually serve us. You know how physical pain works as an alarm? Think about it: we discover the danger of fire, boiling water and sharp objects as children because if we misuse them, we hurt ourselves. In the same way physical pain teaches us what is harmful, feeling very low indeed can help alert us to the fact we might be taking too much on and that we have to look after ourselves, or that we need time to grieve over the loss of a loved one,

or the shock of a traumatic event. **Be kind to yourself, seek support in the shape that works for you and in this way befriend your depressive period; it'll be your best tactic for recovery.** Have you heard the saying, 'Keep your friends close, and your enemies closer'? Bear it in mind, as it describes the approach of this book.

4. This book aims to give you an overview of the various options for managing depression and, where relevant, we've endeavoured to **reflect the guidelines issued by the National Institute for Clinical Excellence (NICE[1]).** It also aims to be as objective as possible about alternative treatments.

5. The format of this book is designed with depression in mind. It's relatively short and comes in bite-sized chunks, (like the sister book to this one, *Making Friends with Anxiety)* because feeling overwhelmed is common when we're depressed and we don't want it to feel more than you can manage. **We could have gone into a lot more detail, but felt it more important to keep it manageable than cover every angle on the subject.** It's worth noting that **the main points are emphasized in bold throughout,** so if you're feeling really wobbly you might like to head for this text as then you'll have less to digest. You'll also find simple exercises entitled 'TRY THIS' and quick tips on recovery throughout the whole book so there are plenty of ways you can actively participate as you read.

---

[1] NICE was set up in 1999 in order to make 'evidence-based recommendations for health and care in England', and there are agreements in place so that the findings are available to those in the rest of the UK.

6. Each chapter focuses on one component of depression to make it easier to find your way around the book. If you've not experienced depression before, we'd advise you to start with Chapters 1 and 2, 'D' for Diagnosis and 'E' for Expert Support, as these will help you work out if you are suffering from depression and introduce the most commonly used treatments. It's here you'll also find tips on how to chat to your doctor about how you're feeling and useful facts about different medications. After that we'll look at ways you can help yourself get through depression by caring for yourself physically, and we'll explore the common thought processes that can perpetuate a depressive state and learn how to challenge them. **Chapter 7 focuses on depression at its most intense, suicidal thoughts and self-harm.** This is followed by an array of suggestions we hope will lift the spirits and help you reconnect with the world. Together the ten chapters make up the word 'D.E.P.R.E.S.S.I.O.N.' – ending with 'N' for 'Next – living in the now'.

7. One of the most distressing aspects of depression is isolation and feeling that you are separate from others and that no one understands. However thousands – nay, *millions* – of people have felt similarly, and because we believe this in itself can be comforting, you'll find quotes throughout this book from people who have also experienced periods of depression. This information was extrapolated from *The Making Peace with Depression Survey*. If you wish to take part too, you can find the survey here: https://goo.gl/forms/81rpFznFi95mWoQI2. Then we can include your feedback in future editions of this book.

8. The peer support doesn't end when you finish this book. It was because I've found the support of fellow sufferers so comforting myself that at the same time I published *Making Friends with Anxiety*, I set up **a group on Facebook** where those with bad anxiety can share experiences and support one another in confidence. You can find the group, called **Making Friends with Anxiety & Depression,** at www.facebook.com/groups/makingfriendswithanxiety[2]. It now has thousands of members and if you suffer from depression, you are welcome to join. Be aware that is NOT mediated by a doctor or

[2]Please note the URL differs from the name of the group.

specialists in mental health so if you are in danger of self-harming right now, please **call an ambulance, go straight to A&E or call the Samaritans free on 116 123**[3] **from any phone to talk,** but it IS a place to share experiences and chat in confidence. The administrators are a fantastic group of volunteers[4] who manage the group in their spare time. They have each experienced poor mental health at some point, and they have also contributed to this book.

'Friendship helps me crawl out of the black hole,' **Lisa**

'We are here for each other,' **Helen**

There is a list of websites and further recommended reading at the end, so by the time you've finished *Making Peace with Depression*, you should have gained a good overview of what can trigger depression and the different treatments available, alongside practical tools, tips and options for ongoing support.

See the book if you will as a companion for people with depression, and reading it as like a chat with a good friend. Like a friend, we may not have *all* the answers, but we will do our best to support you on your journey and out the other side.

[3] Or email jo@samaritans.org
For worldwide suicide hotlines please visit http://www.suicide.org/international-suicide-hotlines.html
[4] Helen Bawden, Carole Clarkson, Danielle Lucas, Karen Palmer, Polly Snaith, Debi Wilson

CONTENTS

1. 'D' is for Diagnosis – do you have depression?

Depression has many potential causes and degrees, and doctors, psychologists and health care professionals use different terms when discussing depressive illness. So let's start by looking at how it feels to be depressed, and explore the difference between depression and sadness. Then we'll look at common symptoms and different kinds of depression.

What exactly is depression?

The way that depression manifests itself is different for each of us and varies day to day. Personally, it's a word I'd use to describe feeling that the world is just 'too much', that all I want to do is lie in bed and hibernate, yet even that is horrible as my thoughts are so negative. This is how I experience more mild depression these days, but I've also experienced much worse depression, where I felt truly awful for several months, lurching from panic to tears and wanting to sleep all the time to insomnia. When I'm this low, it's impossible to work, socialize or generally function.

'It feels as if you will never appreciate the sun again or you are drowning and you have bricks tied around your ankles. Even bird song is like the world laughing at you.' **Charlie**

Should you join the Facebook group I mentioned, you'll soon see, as I have, not just how widespread depression and anxiety are, but also how they impact each of us in a distinct way.

'My depression means that I can switch between feeling high on life and confident and comfortable in myself and my ability, then not ten seconds later and without any logical reason whatsoever, all I feel is down, unmotivated and hopeless. I've had months when I've slept 14-hours-a-day because everything seemed so pointless.' **Dawn**

A clinical definition from Patrick helps clarify: Depression can be described as a mood disorder which gives prolonged feelings of low mood, sadness and negative thinking. It is associated with poor sleep, altered appetite and altered thought processes; they can be too fast or too slow. Depression can cause poor concentration, occasional sensory disturbances such as hallucinations, and in severe cases can lead to suicidal thoughts and plans.

Although considering self-harm to cope with difficult feelings may make you feel better temporarily, self-harm can be dangerous and make your mental state worse in the long run.

'I feel worthless, listless and suicidal. My overwhelming desire is to be alone and not talk to anyone, ever. To sleep to forget. To wish other people ill. I can't see a way out of the black hole, however bright it is outside.' **Leo**

Even if you're only thinking about the idea, these thoughts can feel difficult to control and extremely frightening. I hope as you read you'll find your distress eases and we'll return to this subject in Chapter 7 in more detail. If you're worried about acting on thoughts of self-harm or suicide right now, **please call an ambulance, go straight to A&E or call the Samaritans for free on 116 123 to talk.**

'It's like there's a layer of black cloud in your mind that it is impossible to get past and even the very easiest of tasks is impossible. There's no joy, no happiness, no enjoyment of anything. You are locked in your mind.' **Jez**

Are you depressed or are you just sad?

'Having depression is more than just feeling a bit down; it's a total inability to see beyond how you're feeling at that moment. It's a stupifying, black blanket that sucks the joy out of everything.' **Nick**

Everyone gets down sometimes and situations such as divorce, bereavement and redundancy are painful for almost all of us. So if everyone experiences low mood, when does it become a problem? Here's Patrick again with some pointers.

When we feel sad, a very normal feeling, it tends to be in tune with what is happening around us — times of loss, of struggle or of conflict. **If the sadness becomes prolonged, unmoveable, and is no longer dependent on the various situations life throws at us, however, then depression can be said to occur**.

Still, sometimes a normal sadness, like bereavement, can be extensive. So how long is too long? I'd suggest that **things are beginning to go wrong when your mood is interfering with your ability to function on a day-to-day basis**. For example, is your self-care altered? Are you eating, washing and sleeping as normal? Does your mood affect your ability or desire to work? Does it contribute to lack of enjoyment of usually pleasurable pursuits such as going out with friends, or perhaps sexual intimacy? Have you noticed that you are avoiding friends and social situations?

One of the ways doctors investigate depression is to ask patients to answer a questionnaire that can help measure depression. Do have a look at the PHQ9 test online - you can find it here: http://patient.info/doctor/patient-health-questionnaire-phq-9.[5] How do your score? Does it alter if you do it on different occasions?

If you suspect you have depression, there are many ways forward, and seeing your doctor is only one. **Recognizing that things aren't right is the important first step.**

[5] These questionnaires are copyrighted so can't be reproduced here.

What are the symptoms of depression?

Another way to diagnose depression is to look at the symptoms. Some signs that mood is very low are:

- Poor concentration
- Negativity
- Self-criticism
- A tendency to worry a lot
- A sense of hopelessness
- An inclination to ruminate about the past
- Sadness
- Anxiety and panic attacks
- Lack of self-care (bathing, cleaning the home etc.)
- Drinking too much alcohol, using drugs or smoking more
- Eating too much or too little
- Sleeping too much or too little
- Isolating oneself
- Feeling tired all the time, listless and lacking in energy
- Losing interest in sex
- Experiencing aches and pains with no obvious cause
- Being tearful and crying a lot
- Self-harming or suicidal behaviour

To have one or two of these symptoms doesn't necessarily indicate you are depressed – there can be other reasons for feeling tired or getting aches and pains, for instance, but if you have a lot of these symptoms within a short time frame they may well be signs of depression. You can probably can see that some of them relate to how we **think** and **feel** (we are self-critical and are sad, for instance), some to how we **behave** (self-medicating with alcohol or drugs) and some to the **physical** symptoms (low energy and aches and pains). In *Making Peace with Depression* we'll see how **all of these thought patterns, emotions, behaviours and physical sensations are connected.** Whilst this might sound complicated, it's worth gaining an insight, because **if we tackle one issue we may find other symptoms improve too.** We'll come back to this in Chapter 6.

Different kinds of depression

There are as many forms of depression as there are people on the planet and there is no doubt that sometimes labels can be limiting. Nonetheless, it's useful to be aware of the common terms used by doctors and therapists giving a diagnosis. You may recognize elements of your own experience in the definitions here and gaining clarity can give you a steer as to an appropriate course of action.

Situational Depression is really the same as the sort of extreme sadness we've already touched on, in that it is triggered by a stressful or life-changing event, such as a job loss, the death of a loved one, relationship break-up or trauma. Situational depression is about three times more common than clinical (major) depression, and medications are rarely needed because it tends to clear up over time once the event has ended. However, that doesn't mean it should be ignored, as if the sadness becomes excessive and doesn't go away, it may indicate a major depression.

Clinical (or Major) Depression. It might surprise you to learn that about 7% of the population is experiencing clinical depression right now. If you are clinically depressed, you may feel extremely

sad and hopeless, and have much less energy than normal. You might notice that you have trouble concentrating, are more irritable and there are changes in your sleep or eating habits. You may also have thoughts of death or suicide. If you've had symptoms like these for more than two weeks, or if they come back over and over again for a few days at a time, your first port of call should be your GP or health practitioner. They can formally diagnose you and discuss treatment options and medication.

'Being given the diagnosis of clinical depression let light in, in a weird way, as I had thought everything about me was just wrong. I know people can be against labels, but I feel the opposite; that knowing what you have is helpful – then you can deal with it and manage it. I now believe I suffered from depression as a teenager, and that this was missed by my GP.' **Julie**

Dysthymia is the word used to describe low mood over a long period of time – often a year or more. People can function adequately, but not optimally. Symptoms include sadness, trouble concentrating, fatigue, and changes in sleep habits and appetite.

Postnatal (or Postpartum) Depression is characterized by feelings of extreme sadness, fatigue, loneliness, hopelessness, suicidal thoughts, fears about hurting the baby, and feelings of disconnect from the child. It can occur anywhere from weeks to months after childbirth, and almost always develops within a year after a woman has given birth. Many new mums feel some sadness after their baby is born – but 10-20% of women in the UK develop a mental illness during pregnancy or within the first year after having a baby. It's not just women either: one in eight first-time fathers suffer from depression while their partner is pregnant, according to a survey by scientists at McGill University in Canada.

Premenstrual Dysphoric Disorder (PMDD) affects women during the second half of their menstrual cycle. It is much more severe than Premenstrual Syndrome (PMS) and affects about 5% of women. Symptoms include depression, anxiety and mood swings.

Seasonal Affective Disorder or 'SAD' typically occurs in winter months and is linked to the reduction in natural sunlight. SAD is characterized by symptoms of anxiety, increased irritability, daytime fatigue and weight gain.

Psychotic Depression. According to the National Alliance on Mental Illness, about 20% of people with depression have episodes so severe that they have psychosis, which means that they experience delusions such as paranoia, or see or hear things that are not really there (hallucinate). People with psychotic depression can find it very frightening or upsetting, which may lead them to become catatonic, not speak, or not leave their bed.

Bipolar Disorder. If your periods of extreme lows are followed by extreme highs, you could have Bipolar Disorder (sometimes called Manic Depression as symptoms can alternate between mania and depression). Symptoms of mania include high energy, excitement, racing thoughts and poor judgment and those with Bipolar Disorder may cycle between depression and mania a few times per year or much more rapidly. This disorder affects about 2-3% of the population and has one of the highest risks for suicide.

'I thought anyone with depression was a fruit loop till I experienced it.' **Al**

This is by no means an exhaustive list, but if you suffer from any kind of depressive illness, many of the therapeutic techniques do overlap. In all instances discussing your symptoms with your doctor can help you get the right support, so if you've not been diagnosed your GP should be your first port of call. But before we see how you might approach chatting to your doctor, a quick word from Patrick...

Disease and depression

Living with a chronic disease can contribute significantly to low moods.[6] When I see patients living with common diseases like

[6] There are strong links between physical and mental health problems. Research has found that 30% of people with a long-term physical health problem also have a mental health problem and 46% of people with a mental health

diabetes, heart disease and lung disease I'm in the habit of checking how they are coping, as I know it's often a struggle. Whilst some are fine because they are used to their symptoms and can manage them well, many are not fine and need input as their disease is overwhelming. In some cases patients are at their lowest ebb as their disease has taken over their life and there is little or no pleasure left.

There's a long list of ailments that visibly affect patients, such as the bony distortions of rheumatoid arthritis or the breathlessness of chronic obstructive pulmonary disease, and then there are the multitude of often less visible or stigmatizing illnesses, such as chronic pain, neurological disorders, and some cancers. It can be hard to explain symptoms to family and friends when they can't see them. Pain can come and go, for instance, it can be excruciating and suddenly it can ease off for no apparent reason. These fluctuations are likely to contribute to altered moods and possibly depression. Hopefully your medical teams will be checking up on your mood and assessing how things are going on a regular basis. If you're concerned, you could try the questionnaire mentioned at the start of the chapter. Does it indicate that you need support? Is your mood making your physical illness less tolerable? Consider what might ease the burden for you, and then chat it through with your medical team.

'My experience of depression is complicated because I also have an incurable, degenerative condition (Multiple Sclerosis) which means I am physically disabled and always will be. Experientially, it doesn't feel that the two things are strongly connected however, and my father also suffered from clinical depression so maybe there is a genetic factor.' **Em**

problem also had a long-term physical health problem. https://www.mentalhealth.org.uk/publications/fundamental-facts-about-mental-health-2015

2. 'E' is for Expert Support – getting the right help

Often it's not easy to talk about depression, especially when we're in the midst of a bad bout of it, as our thoughts become tangled and expressing ourselves can seem awfully difficult. According to the National Institute for Mental Health[7] it takes the average person with a mental illness over ten years to ask for help. But you can't expect yourself just to 'get over' depression, any more than you can will yourself to 'get over' a broken leg, and getting support is key to recovery, so let's look at who you can turn to.

Talking with your doctor

If you have depression you may well find it hard to discuss how you are feeling with your friends and family, and the thought of talking to a relative stranger like a doctor can be intimidating. When we are depressed our self-esteem is often low, and this can make us worry about wasting a busy professional's time.

'Doctors are useless. They shoo you away with a "pull yourself together" or "it takes time", all whilst you're sitting there crying your eyes out.' **Pat**

I would be lying if I didn't acknowledge that some doctors aren't that receptive to patients with mental health problems. I have had my share of brusque and unsympathetic GPs too, but please don't be put off. Although when we are depressed these first steps to getting help can seem insurmountable, the vast majority of those who took part in the 'Making Peace with Depression' survey said they found their GPs helpful and understanding, so take it one step at a time. **There is no shame in admitting you need professional help - it's not a sign of weakness, or failure.** If you have issues with one doctor, ask the receptionist if there is a GP at your practice with an interest in mental health, and make an appointment with them.

'My GP is very kind and understanding. I feel reassured after a visit, I never feel that I've been a bother.' **Lucia**

---

[7] Ted Talk https://www.facebook.com/TEDEducation/videos/1247725631907307/

'It took me a while to find a doctor who was sympathetic. A lot of doctors seem incapable and insensitive when dealing with mental health issues and just want to push pills on you.' **Sherman**

Your doctor is there to help you, and a good relationship with your GP can make a big difference to your recovery, so it's worth pausing to consider how to best deal with the encounter. Here are some pointers from Patrick.

How to get the most from an appointment

If you're depressed I feel it's important to seek the help of your GP even though this may feel like the last thing you want to do. There are the problems of having to phone up to make an appointment, getting to the practice, then having to talk through intimate worries with someone you may not have met before who is limited for time.

Although it may feel hard, some planning can be really helpful for both you and your GP. Jot down a couple of notes to get started. 'I haven't been feeling myself for a while.' 'Things are awful.' 'I don't know what's going on, but I can't carry on like this.' These statements will quickly alert your doctor to what's happening and should make it easier for both of you to talk freely. In addition:

1. See the right doctor – do you have a GP you particularly like? Or do you *not* want a specific doctor because of previous problems? In either case, tell the receptionist when you book your appointment. It may mean you have to wait a little longer to see the doctor of your choice, but it's important you feel as comfortable as possible when discussing emotional issues.

2. Consider asking someone to come with you to support you. Is there a friend or family member you trust? If you'd like them to, you can ask if they can come into the appointment with you. It may be that you would prefer to see the doctor on your own so you can speak more freely, but nonetheless having someone with you while you wait can help make a trip to your GP less distressing.

3. Make a list. If you're worried you won't remember all your symptoms and worries, write them down – even ones you think aren't relevant. The body can have strange ways of expressing itself.

4. Tell the GP what you think may be going on. It helps establish your concerns around your symptoms and you can also be reassured if you are worried unnecessarily. However, if you think you may have something more serious then tell the doctor too e.g. family histories of diseases. These vital clues help to build a picture.

5. Allow the GP to ask you questions, even if they seem irrelevant. They are sifting information to make sure there are no physical conditions linked to your low mood. Depression can be triggered by hypothyroidism, B12 deficiency and hormone changes, for instance.

6. Discuss the options. This may involve taking blood tests, trying medication or a referral for counselling, or a combination of these. Which route would you like to try? Tell them. If your GP doesn't know what you're hoping for, they may assume other ways forward.

7. Make a follow up appointment to see how the changes have gone. Changes take time - so wait at least 2-3 weeks before checking in. If you've been prescribed antidepressants they will take 4-6 weeks to take effect, so you may be asked to leave it longer.

Finally, if you feel you didn't connect with your GP, try not to be discouraged. It may be nothing to do with you — it could be have been the consultation before yours involved something so upsetting that they couldn't concentrate. It may be that they're not as aware of mental health issues as they could be. It may be that they should retire! Remember, your doctor is there to support you. They can't fix your life, but most GPs do aim to listen to your worries and provide guidance to the best of their abilities, and you can always ask to see a different doctor next time. **Sarah has made a video of these tips which you can view at https://youtu.be/icHQ-wAEeGs.**

'My doctor is great. She told me depression comes in waves and the waves would be further and further apart. I found that hugely helpful.' **Chris**

'My GP is very understanding. He offered me drugs, which I didn't take, and sessions with a counsellor to help me understand my depression. I found these invaluable and I'm many steps further towards recovery.' **Jin**

<u>**To take medication or not to take medication?**</u>

Treatment for depression usually involves a combination of medicines, talking therapies and self-help, and when you see your doctor, he or she may suggest medication, so it is worth having a think about the prospect before you go.

'SSRIs made me feel numb and spaced out, but they did the job as I stopped wanting to kill myself.' **Sam**

Many people feel ambivalent about taking medication for depression and are reluctant to take antidepressants, in particular. I was so against the idea myself that I struggled through two major depressions without any medication at all. When it came back for a third time, I had to admit my depression wasn't going to go away just because I wanted it to, and I was desperate not to be so ill again so soon. It was at this point that a friend of mine, Niccy, suggested I might give antidepressants a try. 'They helped me a lot,' she said. 'What are you so frightened of?' I told her I thought they might change my personality. 'Do I seem any different to you?' she asked. 'I'm on them now.' I thought about it – the truth was she seemed *more* herself than she had when I'd seen her a few months earlier, when she'd been off work with depression. The woman before me was smiling and able to empathize; before she'd been distraught, withdrawn and self-absorbed. 'No,' I admitted. 'You seem a lot better.' 'So why punish yourself when you don't have to?' Niccy urged. 'But I feel I should be able to manage on my own,' I protested. 'You wouldn't refuse to take medication if you had high blood pressure,' she continued. 'What's the difference?'

It was a useful conversation. Whilst I don't believe medication is right for everyone and nor do I feel it's by any means always necessary, in retrospect I feel some of my own reluctance was connected to the stigma of mental illness – I was *embarrassed* to admit that I needed that level of help. **There shouldn't be**

embarrassment or shame about taking medication for depression — it's not a sign of weakness or shortcoming, so if it's pride that's holding you back, then I'd invite you to ask yourself similar questions to the ones Niccy asked me. After all, it's unlikely we'd berate ourselves in the same way if were we prescribed an anticoagulant for a heart condition or insulin for diabetes, and **a refusal to take medication can be yet another way we beat ourselves up**. You may *still* decide to not to take prescription drugs and if you can manage to recover without, that's great. But they can help, especially, I have found, when used in conjunction with talking therapy, self-help and peer support, all of which we'll come onto presently. Before that here's Patrick with more on medication.

Medication, the options in a nutshell

The medical profession used to be guilty of trying to fix depression with just a pill but now, if you look at the NICE guidelines on depression, they spend much time talking about supportive care and clear management plans before turning to medication[8] — I hope we doctors are getting better! Whilst medication is possibly not going to work on its own, it may help in some circumstances.

1. Selective serotonin reuptake inhibitors, often known as SSRIs, are the most commonly used antidepressants. They are also used for anxiety, and the combinations of anxiety and depression. They may help as part of a management programme by stabilizing your mood, stopping the extreme swings from feeling OK to dropping like a stone, and during counselling and/or therapy they may help you to address deeper issues that are painful to talk through by taking the edge off, softening the blows.

There are several SSRIs, and **finding the right one for you may take time**. Don't despair if it's not the first one. Common drugs are fluoxetine (usually given to younger patients), citalopram (not for those with heart problems) and sertraline. Sertraline tends to have the least interactions with other medication so is usually the first choice for those on several tablets for other conditions.

---

[8] https://www.nice.org.uk/guidance/cg90/chapter/1-guidance#care-of-all-people-with-depression

SSRIs are usually taken once daily in the morning, and they can take between two to four weeks to start working, sometimes longer. (Sarah says they took six weeks to work for her.) This illustration shows in very simple terms how they work:[9]

Whilst it's not 100% clear how SSRIs work, it seems something like this. Imagine your brain is like a bath, and serotonin like water. When you're on an even keel, there's plenty of water, so you can bathe whenever you want.

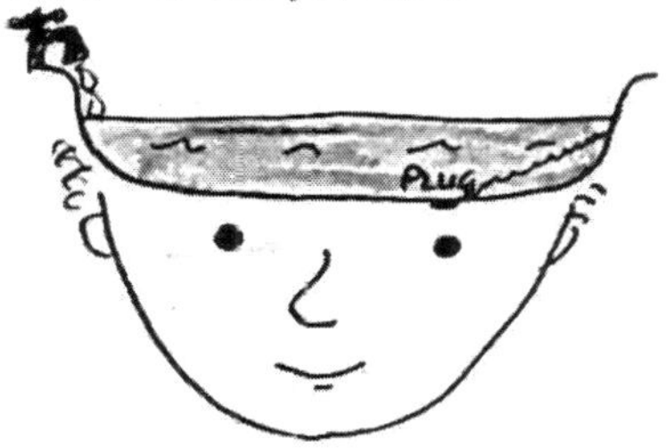

If we let the plug out, it's not a problem, as the serotonin will soon fill the bath again. But when we're depressed, our bodies don't produce enough serotonin, so once we let the plug out, there's no water to refill the bath again.

SSRIs act like a plug; they stop the 're-uptake' of serotonin. Gradually the levels build up again, as serotonin builds up once more in the brain. This is why it takes a while for SSRIs to work; in the same way it takes time for a bath to fill up.

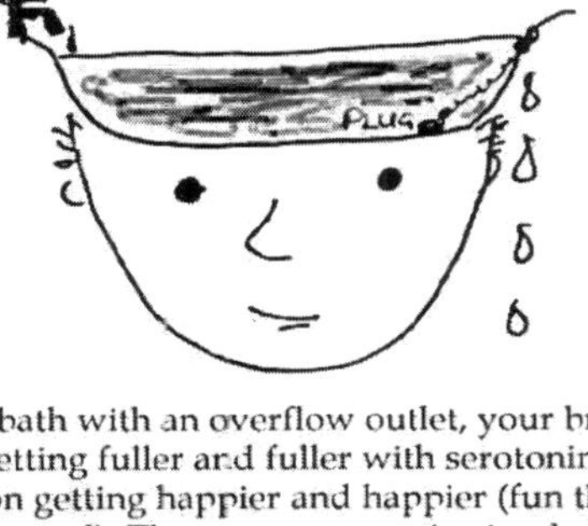

Like a bath with an overflow outlet, your brain doesn't keep getting fuller and fuller with serotonin. You don't carry on getting happier and happier (fun though that might sound). The excess serotonin simply flows away.

---

[9] Dr Tim Cantopher uses a similar analogy in his book, *Depressive Illness: The Curse of the Strong*. Ihis video explains the action in a little more detail. https://www.youtube.com/watch?v=G4r3qCkLUDQ

This can seem frustratingly slow. Unfortunately, the side effects are quick to make their presence felt! Some people get none; some a lot. Nausea is to be expected and should pass, but if the tablets make you very sick, then it's OK to stop them early on – in general, **changing between medications is easier within the first two months of treatment**. However, after a few weeks your body will have got used to them, so **if you've been taking your medication for longer than three or four months your GP will want to withdraw it slowly** before switching you onto something different.[10]

2. Serotonin noradrenaline reuptake inhibitors (SNRIs) and atypical antidepressants are alternatives to SSRIs and tend to be used as a second line. They work in different ways, so may suit some people more. They can also be used if someone has been on an SSRI for a while but the benefits have worn off.

The commonly used SNRIs are venlafaxine and duloxetine. By blocking both the reuptake of serotonin and noradrenaline – the hormone that can make you ready to run from threat, or just very anxious - they can offer a further way of treating depression, or a mixture of anxiety and depression. Again they can have side effects, and if you are prescribed venlafaxine you should have an ECG and blood pressure check first to make sure you don't have heart problems that could be made worse by the medication.

Another common alternative drug is mirtazapine. This is usually used for those troubled by insomnia. It is also used in eating disorders as it can stimulate appetite in higher doses. Mirtazapine can give a good night's sleep but some people feel groggy the next day, and some people get no sleep at all! It can work quicker than the other antidepressants, so is useful in stressful situations such as post-traumatic stress disorder and depression with terminal illnesses.

3. Tricyclic antidepressants are the common older-fashioned drugs that are still used to treat depression when nothing else is working. They were widely used in the 1960s and 1970s before SSRIs came

[10] If you'd like to find out more about coming off antidepressants there's more information here: http://www.mims.co.uk/antidepressants-guide-switching-withdrawing/mental-health/article/882430

along. Although they work well, it's their prominent side effects that limit their use. Drugs like lofepramine, amitriptyline and nortriptyline are the commonest ones. Some people take these drugs for other indications such as to prevent migraine or to treat nerve pain. They work quickly on mood, and for some people are the ideal choice. However, they can cause dry mouth, blurred vision, constipation, confusion and hallucinations, so you can appreciate why they aren't the ideal first choice!

Dothiepin or dolsulepin is no longer prescribed due to its side effects, but if you are taking it please don't stop suddenly – if you've been stable on it for a while it may be best to stay on. Speak to your doctor about the possibility or need to change.

As you can see, there are many choices in terms of antidepressants, and your doctor may discuss trying one of the above, or switching it depending how it is tolerated. **For any patient, review is essential two to three weeks after starting.**

4. Other medications.

a. Short-term calming medications. Valium or diazepam is great at calming crisis but is highly addictive. Nonetheless, it can be useful in the short-term as it can calm the merry-go-round of thoughts when things feel like they are spinning out of control. It can be used whilst waiting for one of the SSRIs to work for instance. An alternative to this is buspirone, which can also take the edge off anxiety symptoms, but again is only to be used in the short term.

Sleeping tablets like zolpidem or zopiclone can help to get sleep back into normal patterns when depression is disruptive. But after only two weeks you can become dependent on them, so please use sparingly if you are prescribed them.

b. Antipsychotics. When depression is very severe it can cause a loss of normal thinking in the form of hallucinations or confusion — this is known as psychosis. Antipsychotics such as risperidone or quetiapine are useful in these cases. They are very helpful drugs at times of crisis but need careful monitoring, which will be done with a psychiatric team. This means they are not usually prescribed by a GP in the first instance, so we won't go into detail here.[11]

c. Bipolar disorder. When depression is accompanied by unrealistically happy or ecstatic moods it can as debilitating as a psychosis. This fluctuating state is often controlled using lithium[12] or one of the antipsychotic drugs mentioned above. Again, they are usually prescribed by a psychiatrist in the first instance, not a GP.

Your doctor will be able to advise you more fully on the various pharmaceutical alternatives and there's sensible information http://www.nhs.uk/Conditions/Depression/Pages/treatment options.aspx.

In all cases, but especially with antipsychotics and medications for bipolar disorder, **if you're thinking of stopping or changing your medication, be aware that doing so suddenly can provoke a further episode of illness and it's important that you speak to your doctor first.**

'I took dolsulepin for 12 years. It helped calm me down, but I had no energy and felt sedated all the time, so my quality of life was impaired. ***When I came off, my GP gave me no support.*** *Turns out I withdrew too fast – I still have horrible side effects and it's now six years later.'* Pam

[11] More information can be found at http://www.nhs.co.uk/Conditions/Psychosis/Pages/Treatment.aspx
[12] If you are on lithium, please ensure you have your blood lithium levels and kidney function checked at least every six months.

Alternatives to conventional medicine

You may wish to manage your anxiety without the aid of conventional medicine. If so, you could investigate supplements.

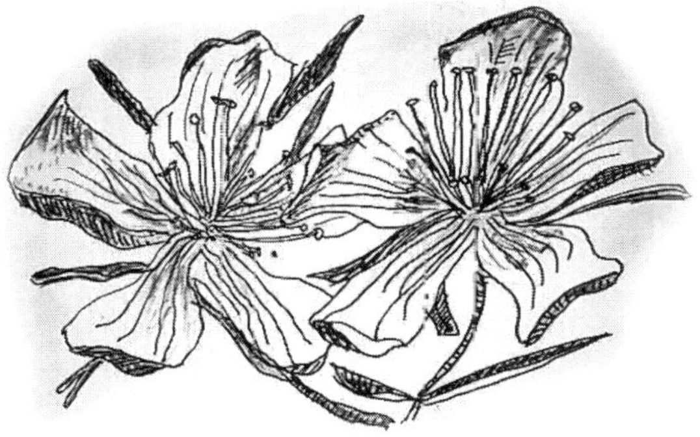

1. St. John's Wort is a herbal remedy that has long been used as an alternative treatment for mood swings, depression, anxiety and insomnia. It is derived from a wild flowering plant called *Hypericum Perforatum*; the leaves and flowers of which are harvested and dried. They can then be brewed in a tea or taken in a pill or liquid form. Scientific studies affirm that while St. John's Wort is effective for treating mild depression, it works no better than a placebo for treating severe depression. One important consideration is that St. John's Wort can reduce the efficacy of other medications[13] including SSRIs, so you'll need to let your doctor know if you are considering it.

2. Omega-3 fatty acids are a type of fat needed for normal brain function. Studies have linked depression with a low intake of omega-3 fatty acids, and preliminary studies suggest that omega-3s taken alongside antidepressants are more effective than antidepressants alone. They are found in cold water fish such as salmon, sardines and anchovies as well as **fish oil** and **cod liver oil**. If you're vegetarian, ground flaxseeds are a good source of omega-3s.

3. Folic Acid is a B vitamin found in green leafy vegetables, fruit, beans, and fortified grains. It is one of the more prevalent vitamin deficiencies due to poor diet and medication such as aspirin and oral contraceptives – it's needed in normal levels for Vitamin B12 to work. Preliminary research suggests that people with depression

[13] It also interacts with other prescribed medication in unexpected ways, says Patrick. It can interfere with the oral contraceptive and epileptic medication, for instance. See www.drugs.com/drug-interactions/st-john-s-wort.html.

who also have low folate levels may not respond as well to antidepressants, and taking folic acid in supplement form may improve the effectiveness of antidepressants.

4. **5-HTP**, or 5-hydroxytryptophan, is produced naturally in the body and is used in the formation of the neurotransmitter serotonin. Although 5-HTP may boost serotonin levels, many experts feel there is not enough evidence to determine its safety[14].

Please bear in mind that all these should be used in addition to – not instead of – seeking medical advice from a doctor, and that self-treating depression and avoiding or delaying standard care may have an impact on your recovery.[15] Moreover **no form of medication, conventional or otherwise, will treat the underlying cause of your depression,** so **the next step is to consider therapy.**

Different kinds of therapy in another nutshell

Twenty odd years ago, when I experienced my first major depression, getting any kind of therapy on the NHS was almost unheard of. Since then there has been a sea change in treatment, and now **some therapies (most often Cognitive Behavioural Therapy or counselling) are available on the National Health** in the UK[16], though waiting times vary depending on where you live. 'Many GPs recommend therapy to start with,' says Patrick. If your depression is quite severe your GP may recommend that you have some form of talking therapy alongside a course of antidepressants – research suggests that a combination of an antidepressant and therapy works better than having just one of these treatments.[17]

---

[14] It should not be combined with antidepressants.

[15] Many herbal products available in the UK are not subject to the same degree of standardization as other medication, which means there may be variability between products or a lack of clarity regarding ingredients. This can also make it difficult to compare trial results. The best way through this confusion is to look out for Traditional Herbal Registration (THR) marking on product packaging. This means the herbal remedy has been assessed against quality standards and you'll have information about how and when to use it. Avoid buying herbal medication online because products manufactured outside the UK may not be subject to regulation.

[16] In 2010 the government announced plans to make psychological therapies widely available on the NHS. This is because they've been shown to be effective treatments for common mental health conditions. The programme is called Improving Access to Psychological Therapies (IAPT). As a result, evidence-based psychological therapies can now be accessed through GP surgeries, the workplace, schools and colleges and some voluntary and charitable organisations.

[17] https://www.mentalhelp.net/blogs/a-combination-of-cognitive-behavioral-therapy-antidepressant-medication-works-best-for-depressed-adolescents/

[18] A good summary: www.nimn.nih.gov/health/topics/pscyhotherapies/index.shtml

What's available through the NHS?

There are many forms of talking therapy[18] but here are the main choices depression sufferers are offered via the NHS:

1. **Counselling** is ideal for people who need help coping with a current crisis, so if you are suffering from 'situational depression' (see Chapter 1) you may well find it helpful — it can be particularly beneficial at times of bereavement. It usually involves 6-12 sessions, each of an hour, where you talk in confidence to a counsellor.

2. **Cognitive behavioural therapy (CBT) aims to help you manage your problems by encouraging you to change the way you think and behave.** It focuses on your current situation and looks for practical ways to improve your state of mind on a daily basis. For moderate depression, NICE recommend computerised cognitive behavioural therapy (CCBT). For more severe depression, one-to-one CBT or group therapy is recommended.

3. **Mindfulness-based cognitive therapy (MBCT)** combines mindfulness techniques like meditation and breathing exercises with cognitive therapy. NICE recommends MBCT to help people avoid repeated bouts of depression.

'If you've ever just burst into tears because it all becomes too much, then that's when you need to start talking to someone.' **Ella**

4. In **group therapy**, up to around 12 people meet, together with a therapist. It's a useful way for people who share a common problem to get support and advice from each other.

5. If you have severe depression, **you may be referred to a mental health team made up of psychologists, psychiatrists, specialist nurses and occupational therapists**. These teams often provide intensive specialist talking treatments as well as prescribed medication.

6. Electroconvulsive therapy (ECT) is very occasionally used in cases of severe or life-threatening depression. This involves being given an anaesthetic then receiving an electrical 'shock' to your brain. It is not suitable for everyone but it can be effective when antidepressants and all other treatments have not worked.

The chart below shows that the majority of those who responded to the 'Making Peace with Depression' survey have had some form of talking therapy, most commonly Cognitive Behavioural Therapy (CBT). Many have tried more than one kind, although not all of these are available on the NHS.

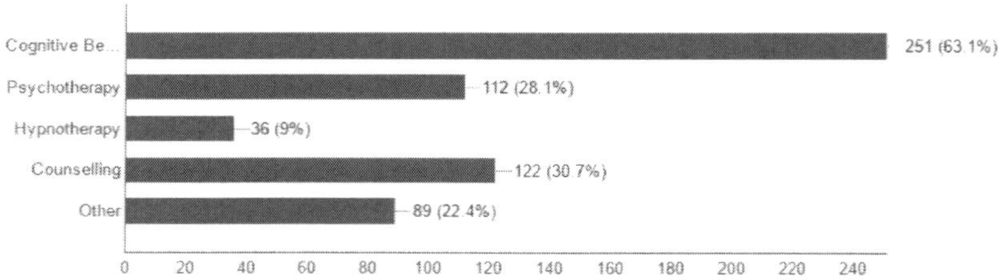

Many of our survey respondents found talking therapy helpful:

'CBT helped me get everything into perspective and think over the events that led to my crisis. It helped me build a more constructive model of how to view it all, and how to view myself too.' **Ben**

Often the success of therapy is down to the relationship between the individual and the therapist:

'I would say if you don't find your therapist is helping after four sessions, then don't be afraid to speak up and ask for a different one.' **Herman**

Other respondents felt therapy terminated too soon:

'My counselling was limited to six sessions – nowhere near enough.' **Su**

The latter comes down to budget – generally it costs the NHS less to prescribe medication than it does therapy.

In other countries such as the United States, the health system is very different. Please consult your health care provider to find out what your policy covers.

What about therapy outside the NHS?

If you are lucky enough to have medical insurance, you may find therapy is covered by your policy so it's worth phoning your insurer to see if your condition is covered. I agree it's unfair, but if so, you may get help more quickly than through the NHS.

'I was told the waiting list for CBT through the NHS was a year where I live, so when I discovered I could have regular group therapy through my insurance, you can imagine it was a big relief.' **Mags**

Alternatively, you may decide you wish to **consult a therapist privately**. The advantage to this is that if you can afford it, you can decide what kind of therapy you wish to have, who you want to see and how many sessions you'd like. To help ensure you see a reputable practitioner, do some homework: you'll find The British Psychotherapy Foundation is a useful resource of UK-accredited psychotherapists, as is the British Association of Behavioural and Cognitive Psychotherapies. Details are on page 126.

'NHS CBT was a short-term fix, then I found a psychotherapist privately and he saved my life.' **Alan**

1. Psychotherapy. Compared to counselling or CBT, psychotherapy tends to place more emphasis on talking about how past experiences, such as an unhappy childhood, influence what happens in the present. It also tends to last longer (sessions can continue for a year or more) so is rarely available on the NHS. There are dozens of different schools of psychotherapy and evidence as to how much it can help with depression is debated. Some argue that because people with depression tend to ruminate a lot (something we'll talk about in Chapter 4), it can encourage negative thinking and be unhelpful. Personally, I found it helped me see when echoes of past experiences were reverberating in present situations and making my sense of anxiety and/or depression worse. But I'm not you, and deciding if you should pursue it is not something I can do on your behalf.

2. Complementary therapies. From aromatherapy to yogic breathing, there many alternative techniques used to tackle depression. Some find massage helps to calm them, others have experienced benefit from Reiki healing, and I've found acupuncture very helpful myself. Unfortunately there isn't space in this book to examine these in detail, but if you feel motivated to do your own research, we'd keenly encourage it.[16]

---

[16] One issue with alternative therapies is how to sort the charlatans from the conscientious practitioners. Conventional medicine is controlled by statutory regulation to help ensure that doctors are properly qualified and adhere to certain codes of practice, but other professions are not so rigorously regulated. Your safest bet is to check that your therapist is registered with an organisation that is itself registered with the Professional Standards Authority – as is the case for anyone listed with the Complementary and Natural Healthcare Council or the British Acupuncture Council. Other professional associations hold membership lists or registers of practitioners of specific complementary and alternative medicines, such as the British Homeopathic Association, The Reiki Association and the UK Register of Chinese Herbal Medicine. On the whole I'd say that, if a treatment is working for you and you can afford it, continue, because your wellbeing is the most important thing of all.

Helping yourself

Whatever your circumstance, I understand all too well that if you're feeling depressed to have to wait for medication to work or for a therapeutic assessment can seem torture. I also appreciate that lots of us can't afford to pay for therapy, and not everyone has medical insurance. Don't lose hope. Please trust me because I've been there: you *will* get better, not least because **there's a huge amount you can do to help yourself. Even though you might not feel like it right now, *you* hold the key to your own recovery. Moreover, much of the advice that follows over the next few chapters draws upon techniques used in CBT, MBCT and psychotherapy anyway, and should stand you in good stead whether or not you consult a professional.**

Kate agrees that a combination of approaches is often needed. 'Talking therapies can leave you feeling raw: I've found that if I'm low, I need medication to get me into a place where I can consider making the changes I need to get me out of the hole. But at other times, I've spotted the signs soon enough to get myself feeling brighter just by looking after myself better.'

So let's crack on with seeing how you can help yourself slide along the mood scale and feel happier, because that's something we can work on together right away.

3. 'P' is for Physical Illness – the mind/body connection

So far, we've mainly been talking about depression in terms of our thoughts and feelings. Certainly, it's usually described as a 'mental' illness. But our emotions don't exist in a vacuum, and to see depression purely as a disease of the mind is simplistic. Depression doesn't just affect mood, nor is it simply a question of behavioural symptoms – it has an impact on us physically.

Changes in the brain

Depression has physical manifestations in the brain and is associated with smaller frontal lobes and hippocampal volumes. On a more micro scale, **depression is associated with the abnormal transmission or depletion of brain messengers called neurotransmitters, in particular serotonin, noradrenaline and dopamine**. It's also linked to blunted Arcadian rhythms or changes in the REM part of the sleep cycle and hormone irregularities such as high cortisol and deregulation of thyroid hormones.[17] **These changes in the brain have a knock-on effect;** serotonin and noradrenaline pathways also travel down into the spinal cord serving the rest of the body, for example, which can in turn alter our pain threshold. This means we become more sensitive to pain, and may make us likely to succumb to viruses like colds and flu.

Common ways depression impacts us physically

'I want to sleep all the time and have no energy.' **Russell**

'It's almost like I'm not in my own body.' **Carmen**

- Of all the signs that depression is felt in the body as well as our thoughts, the most prevalent is physical pain. Increased aches and pains occur in about 2/3 people with depression.[18]
- Chronic fatigue – energy loss is often so overwhelming that movement becomes arduous. It can even grind to a halt.

[17] https://www.youtube.com/watch?v=z-IR48Mb3W0
[18] According to one study, people with fibromyalgia are more than three times more likely to have major depression than people without fibromyalgia

- Cardiovascular problems — those who have heart attacks are more likely to become depressed, and people with depression may be more susceptible to heart attacks.[19]
- Insomnia, lack of deep sleep or oversleeping — nearly all depression sufferers experience sleep problems.[20]
- Decreased interest in sex
- Decreased or increased appetite
- Decreased memory
- Digestive problems — IBS, bloating, constipation
- Migraine

The complexities of diagnosis

In Chapter 1 we discussed how some health conditions make depression much more likely and undiagnosed conditions like hypothyroidism or B12 deficiency can cause depression as a symptom. Treatment for those conditions may lead to an improvement in mood and many other physical problems, like low energy and sleep disruption. Nonetheless these complexities, coupled with the fact that depression can also have somatic[21] symptoms of its own, can make diagnosis difficult. **When patients present physical symptoms along with mood-related changes it can be hard for doctors to be certain where the issues originate**.

Many years ago I made an appointment with my doctor because my foot was sore; numbness had been troubling me for several weeks. It was only when I burst into tears and said everything was 'getting on top of me' that my GP clicked that maybe something deeper was amiss. Interestingly, a while later when she came to the launch of my first novel, she confessed to me that she was no longer working full time, and that she'd been under great stress then herself. 'I saw myself in you,' she said, 'which is probably why I knew.' It's a handy reminder that doctors are human too.

---

[19] http://www.secondopinion-tv.org/episode/heart-disease-depression

[20] 80% complain of insomnia, another 15% sleep excessively.

[21] Relating to the body, as distinct from the mind.

'My depression took the form of overwhelming despair along with physical symptoms like loss of appetite that I now know were connected.' **Jon**

The way forward

Many antidepressants can help relieve somatic symptoms, but some drugs work more robustly than others, so if you're in a lot of physical discomfort, it's worth discussing the options with your GP. In terms of helping yourself to heal, please don't be downcast, however ironic that might sound in a book about depression. That it's hard to ascertain cause and effect in relation to symptoms simply underlines it is important to treat depression holistically: in looking after ourselves physically, we can care for our minds and vice versa.

Looking after yourself physically

'As I tend to spend too much time thinking and not enough time doing, I often neglect my body. So any form of exercise or physical therapy that brings me back into my body helps to ground and centre me when I have slipped off my "mental rails" into anxiety and/or depression.' **Em**

The benefits of taking control of your physical health can't be exaggerated. **What we put into our bodies — or avoid — can make a difference to our energy levels and overall wellbeing, and gentle exercise can help boost mood as well as raise our levels of fitness.**

Eating well is associated with fewer mood swings, lower anxiety levels and can reduce pre-menstrual fatigue. Good nutrition is so fundamental to recovery that the basics are worth underlining here in this book, but entrenched dietary habits can be incredibly hard to change.

'My diet was terrible when I had depression; I couldn't summon the energy to cook. I definitely notice a difference in my mood when I eat badly.' **Becca**

One of many frustrating things about the human psyche is our natural tendency, when we're feeling low, to drag ourselves down further still. It's a topic Kate has lots to say about.

Some positive guidelines for eating well

I believe cooking is good for the soul; nourishing, instead of punishing, your body can have physical *and* psychological benefits. Like many sayings, 'you are what you eat' has much truth in it, and if we eat highly processed foods or takeaways, we're likely to feel sluggish and guilty. However, the weariness that often accompanies depression means that the idea of cooking a meal, or even shopping for ingredients, can seem too much. **It's easy to fall into a vicious circle of eating poorly, putting on weight or disrupting our digestive system**, and feeling even more hopeless about our bodies and ability to look after ourselves. **Breaking that cycle can be as simple as preparing a single, healthy meal.** Not only will it taste better, but you'll also feel positive about planning and completing a task that is satisfying and self-nurturing.

TIP: Instead of seeing your body as the enemy, befriend it; nourish it and show it gratitude for supporting you along the way.

One of the things I've learned by discussing food and dietary habits with thousands of people is that there's no single perfect approach that works for everyone. Our genes, our early childhood and even the current state of our gut bacteria all influence how food affects our body and mind (more on the fascinating science of our microbiome shortly). But here are simple guidelines to help you create healthy eating habits. If you feel your diet is lacking, **it's worth thinking about focusing on one of these areas at a time, rather than changing everything overnight.**

- **Base your meals around fresh produce**: vegetables and fruit are high in fibre, filling, and when you eat different varieties, provide lots of the micronutrients the body needs to function well. Preparing meals from fresh produce also means you're in control of how they're cooked, as well as how much salt or what kind of fat is added. Don't forget frozen and canned vegetables can be cheaper than fresh but preserve the vitamins and minerals.
- **Cut back on processed foods**: convenience foods are exactly that – convenient – but transporting and preserving prepared meals often means nutritional value is lost, and unfamiliar additives are introduced to ensure longer shelf-lives. Factories are also trying to cater to all so the levels of salt or spice they add may not suit you.
- **Shop and eat seasonally**: seasonal produce tastes better – think of strawberries, at their juiciest in July – and is cheaper to buy. It's also usually at its most nutritious. Learn to celebrate the seasons.
- **Eat widely**: variety doesn't only stop us getting bored, it also helps us consume diverse nutrients. For example, the idea of 'eating a rainbow' of different coloured fruit and veg helps you get a range of natural 'phytonutrients' that support good health.
- **Find good sources of protein**: protein is one of the three macronutrients – it helps the body repair itself, and create the enzymes and hormones we need to function and that can affect mood. Look for varied sources of protein in your diet: if you eat meat, don't ban red meat but balance it out with dairy foods (e.g. cheese and yogurt), eggs and pulses (lentils, beans, and soya products like tofu).

- **Don't avoid 'good fats'**: the very low-fat regimes of the last few decades are hard to sustain, and the evidence for their effects on heart health is now debated, and often disputed. We also know that low intake of omega-3 fatty acids has been linked to depression (see page 33). The Mediterranean diet, which is high in vegetables, pulses and olive oil but includes some dairy, is protective against cardiovascular disease[22] and may protect against depression[23]. Fat is higher in calories than the other nutrients but it is also satisfying and improves how food tastes. So use controlled amounts of fats with minimal processing – extra-virgin olive oil and butter rather corn oil or margarine.
- **Avoid too much sugar and too many processed carbs**: despite the many much-hyped diets, carbs are not the enemy. Carbs are just how plants store their energy BUT processing does have a huge influence on their effect on the body. Choose 'whole' foods – wholegrain breads and grains like brown rice; mostly whole fruits rather than smoothies and juices; and less 'pure' sugar in sauces, cakes and sweets.
- **'Free-from' doesn't automatically mean healthier:** a small number of people need to avoid gluten or lactose (a form of dairy sugar) due to diagnosed health conditions like Coeliac disease. But the replacements – gluten-free breads, for example – aren't necessarily healthier or lower in calories. If you suspect certain foods of causing health problems, try cutting back a little, and see if you feel better. If your symptoms are severe, see your doctor.

- **Stay hydrated:** the body (and brain) need to be well-hydrated to function well, but busy lives and irregular eating can dehydrate us

[22] https://www.ncbi.nlm.nih.gov/pmc/articles/PMC2684076/
[23] https://www.ncbi.nlm.nih.gov/pubmed/23636545

(we get a lot of water from our food). Keep a water bottle nearby, and aim for two litres but don't fret if you don't make it. It stands to reason that needs vary depending on our size and activity levels – if you're cycling the Tour de France you're going to need more than I do sitting at my desk typing this.

In summary, aim for balance, and prioritise 'real' ingredients and food that's as unprocessed as possible: writer Michael Pollan summed it up brilliantly: EAT FOOD, NOT TOO MUCH, MAINLY PLANTS.

The A-word – appetite, disordered eating and weight

Before the recipes, a quick word about appetite. Appetite – the urge to eat – is a fundamental process, but one that can be severely affected by our mood. Whether it's the loss of appetite that many of us notice in the early stages of depression, or a desire for comforting or sugary foods, what we eat is driven by much more than an empty stomach.

Eating well isn't just about *what we eat, it's also about how we eat*. It's worth paying attention to eating habits and triggers, especially if depression seems to be accompanied by disordered eating e.g. bingeing or putting on weight. Here are some tips:

- **Make eating an occasion**: even if you're eating alone, set the table or make up a nice tray with your favourite crockery. Take a little time to arrange the food, add some salad to the plate, and a lemon slice to your water. Small moments of calm, especially over familiar rituals, can be a great solace during dark days.
- **Eat mindfully**[24]**:** take time to savour the smell of your meal, how it appears, the colours on the plate. Just looking at food we like starts off the digestive process. And chew each mouthful, rather than gobbling – leave that to the turkeys of the planet! Put your cutlery down. Enjoy the experience. It takes time to feel full or 'satiated' – eating more slowly helps avoid overeating.
- **If you're concerned about over-eating, and feel the urge to eat outside regular mealtimes, ask yourself if you're really hungry, or thirsty, or emotional**. Write notes to see if there's a pattern.

[24] We'll talk more of mindfulness in Chapter 4 and Chapter 10.

- **If you do overdo it, be kind to yourself.** One meal won't make you put on weight long-term, or damage your body. Forgive yourself and move on.
- **Give thanks for your food.** I practise intermittent fasting, eating only one or two meals two days each week, and it has helped me feel grateful and more in control of eating. Making any kind of conscious choice around food and adopting better habits can be hugely helpful. We'll talk more about this in Chapter 7.

Looking ahead: could 'friendly bacteria' tackle low mood and depression?

Isn't it interesting how often we describe emotions as located in our gut? Take the expressions 'butterflies in my tummy', 'gut instinct' and 'having a bellyful', say. And now developments in genetic research are revealing profound connections between our digestive systems and mental health.

Like most of us, I can be a bit squeamish about creepy crawlies, but I find the science of exploring our 'microbiome' – the many billions of bacteria that live on our skin and inside our bodies – strangely fascinating. It's revealing that we are only '10% human' – 90% of the genetic material on and in our bodies belongs not to us but to bacteria that have been colonising people since we first emerged from the swamps. Imagine! Those organisms affect how our body behaves in countless ways – from the calories we absorb from food, to how vulnerable we are to infection, and whether we'll go on to develop cancer or diabetes. But for those of us who suffer from periods of poor mental health, **the most exciting work is around the connection between our digestion and our brains**. This 'gut-brain axis' is the focus of much research, as it's believed that gut microbes can send messages to the central nervous system. This can affect levels of serotonin and tryptophan, which influence our moods, and are also targeted by antidepressants.

It's thought that by altering the balance of bacteria present in our digestive systems (up to 100 trillion of them) and encouraging more

of those that produce positive effects, we may be able to develop new treatments for anxiety and depression. Animal studies have shown much higher levels of stress hormones (e.g. cortisol) in mice with gut microbes, compared to specially bred 'germ-free' mice, suggesting that our microbes influence our response to difficult events. Small-scale trials of adults and children given probiotic supplements (containing different specially isolated bacteria), have also shown increased concentration and reduced anxiety compared to groups given a placebo. It's early days – and we can't yet take a pill or eat a yogurt that guarantees to improve our mood. But eating a varied diet, full of different produce and lots of vegetables high in fibre, will promote diversity in your gut. And though you may like to take probiotics, eating live yogurt (many manufacturers are now listing the bacteria they contain) may be cheaper and just as good. Watch out for exciting developments in this field – and take it as further proof that **our mental health is definitely not 'all in the mind'. We should never blame ourselves for experiencing depression**.

The value of physical exercise

Exercise effectively:

- Burns off stress hormones such as adrenaline
- Tires your muscles, reducing excess energy and tension
- Forces healthier breathing
- Reduces feelings of frustration and anger
- Improves sleeping, physical health and the immune system
- Provides distraction from worries and improves mood
- Releases brain chemicals (endorphins) which are natural antidepressants

What's more, **exercise is free, you can control your own timetable and you'll feel physically stronger and fitter if you participate**. Given these benefits, it's amazing every public footpath across the land isn't crowded with people suffering from depression taking their daily constitutional. Fitness classes and cycle lanes should be heaving with people like you and me, all hoping to burn off the blues along with the calories. Yet all too often when we're low, exercise is the *last* thing we feel like doing. We want to cocoon ourselves on the sofa and eat chocolate. Depression depletes energy and the prospect of going for a jog can feel as difficult as pushing water uphill with a sieve – probably why 35% of respondents to our survey said they did under an hour of exercise a week.

'I'm tired, always tired.' **Ali**

'I go walking if I feel positive – otherwise I get scared of being alone.' **Jean**

Let me confess that I'm no gym bunny either. When I've been depressed, I've found it hard to get out of bed, let alone be energetic. My motivation to do *anything* went out of the window. If you can't face any form of exercise at the moment, for now just let the notion of doing a few minutes a day begin to percolate and we will return to the subject of motivation in Chapter 9. If you can manage it however, try to envisage the healthier, more vital you that lies deep below the layers of despair. That person is still there, keen to emerge into the daylight.

TIP: Start small. Even going up and down the stairs half a dozen times or a walk round the block can break the cycle of lethargy.

Befriend yourself and be gentle with your psyche. A light jog can boost mood; spraining an ankle will have the reverse effect.

'Going to the gym has made a huge difference. I am more confident. It was hard at first, to talk to people. I kept at it, made friends, had a laugh, got fit, and it's helped my mental health a lot. I never thought I'd see the day when I enjoy it, but now I do.' **Peter**

'Exercise' doesn't just mean sports. **Any pastime that requires you to be physically active can benefit your mental health** – so gardening, walking the dog, and doing some DIY or brisk housework all count.

4. 'R' is for Reaction – learning to respond differently

The way we react to other people, events and experiences can be a big factor in depression. Becoming more aware of our common thought patterns and learning to challenge them can help reduce overwhelm, and learning to be more objective about how others see us and trying to be less tough on ourselves is also useful.

The cycle of negativity

One of the most useful insights I gained from CBT was that **people with depression are prone to thinking in certain ways**. Common thoughts include:

- 'It would have been better if…' – going over and over past events and ruminating
- 'I should have done…' – negative, self-critical thoughts
- 'I can't do it' – pessimism
- 'It's all too much' – overwhelm
- A sense of unreality and disconnect from others
- Increased sensitivity to criticism
- An inability to concentrate
- A desire to self-harm (which we'll come onto in Chapter 7)

Some of us are more inclined to certain thoughts than others, nonetheless depressed people share a common tendency to criticize and berate ourselves, tell ourselves we're failures and useless. These thoughts can create **feelings** such as:

- Sadness
- Loneliness
- Worry
- Guilt
- Shame
- Anger
- Frustration
- Apathy
- Vulnerability

- Powerlessness
- A sense of rejection
- Numbness
- Emptiness
- Regret

Feeling like this is awful, which tends to compound depression.

Common patterns of thinking in those with depression

What's interesting is that depressed people aren't just inclined to similar negative thoughts, but the way we think tends to follow similar patterns, too. For example:

- **Black-and-white or all-or-nothing thinking – when we polarize outcomes into extremes** – is something depressed people are very susceptible to. We see ourselves as *complete* failures, *totally* un-loveable, *never* likely to be happy again and so on. (I'm sure you can fill in your own examples here.) We become prone to filtering out information that might make us perceive situations with greater subtlety, missing out on the full spectrum of events and experiences.

- **Over generalizing – evidence is extrapolated from an experience and an unjustified conclusion is drawn**. This is a form of mental filtering, because we only allow negative information into our minds and ignore positive information. Thus we tell ourselves 'bad things are always happening to me', 'I never meet decent men/women' and so forth.

- **Self-blame** – situations are interpreted as reflecting something negative about you when they may have nothing to do with you. When we're low we often assume we can read other people's minds, intentions and motives and so we end up thinking 'She's not very chatty, I must have done something to upset her', for instance.
- **Commanding the self** – we're always saying 'I should do x' and 'I must finish y'; barking internal instructions at ourselves. This means we're continually setting ourselves impossible goals which then weigh us down.
- **Catastrophizing or fortune telling** – we exaggerate a threat or the likelihood of a negative outcome occurring, thinking 'they're late home, they must have had an accident' or 'what's the point in trying? It won't work out'.

'I felt like the person who was having all these dark thoughts was someone completely "other" than me. She had different thoughts, different character traits, different obsessions. I didn't recognise myself in her at all. I would wake up in the middle of the night scared of my own brain, in a sense; I didn't know where these thoughts had come from and, because it didn't feel like it was me having them, I felt like I had no control of them and no idea how far they would go.' **Rebecca**

Given such frightening experiences and a strong tendency for pessimism, it's unsurprising depressed people often assume if we have one bad day, dozens of other bad days will follow. The irony is that **this belief serves to reinforce the experience, so gloom becomes a self-fulfilling prophecy**. As such it's a classic example of a 'thinking error' — an irrational pattern of thinking that can cause us to feel bad and sometimes act in self-defeating ways. When I realized one bad day didn't *necessarily* lead to another it was a revelation; from then on I was able to see that a period of depression might be a more temporary state rather than a fast track to an eternity of hell. On bad days I still find it hard to convince myself things could get better soon, but I'm less inclined to see my state of mind as permanent because I've discovered that if I am open and self-aware, **change is possible.**

Changing our minds

It wasn't always this way. I used to be convinced there was nothing I could do to change my thinking, let alone my emotions. I believed that my thoughts controlled me, rather than the other way round. Now I've come to understand that the opposite is true – **we *can* influence our thoughts, and if we change the way we think, then our mood will lift and, eventually, depression will diminish too**.

'But I *feel* it, so it must be true,' I can hear you protest. I know where you're coming from. 'I think therefore I am,' is a tenet of western philosophy; I was sure that my thoughts were what made me, me, and without them my sense of self would disappear.

What happens when we panic

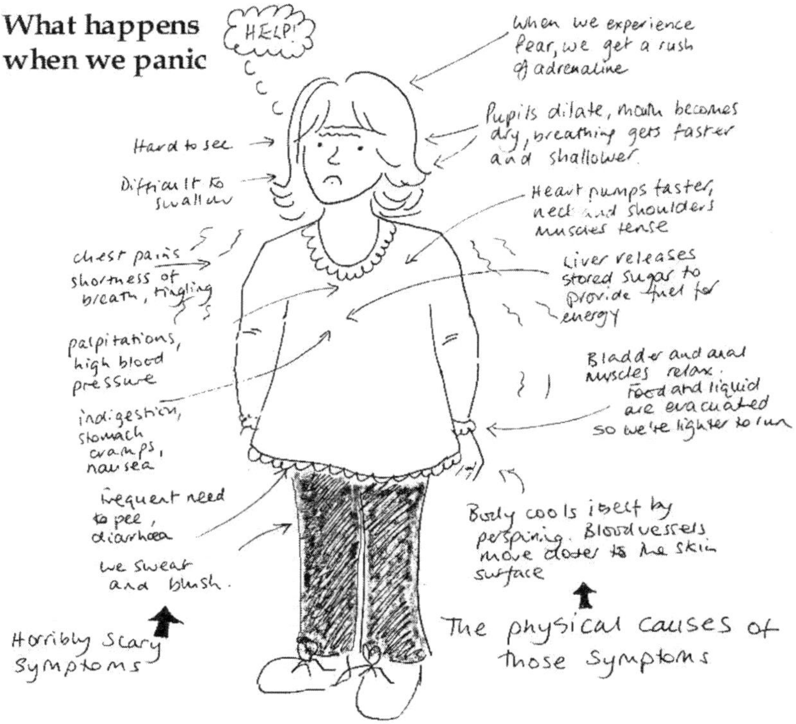

Certainly when I was mid breakdown, it felt like my brain was out of control, my thoughts were spinning so fast. It was terrifying, so then I would panic, and with that release a bucket full of adrenaline, and end up with the shed load of physical and mental symptoms that often come with anxiety (see illustration). The upshot was I'd feel even worse. Anxiety and depression can trigger one another, and like me, you may suffer from both. Over half of those who experience depression also experience symptoms of anxiety.[25] If you've severe anxiety you'll find more detail in *Making Friends with Anxiety*, but I don't want you to feel you *have* to read that book as well as this one, so I've included the salient points which relate to depression here.

Making friends with anxiety and depression

Arguably **the single most important thing to grasp about anxiety is that because it is related to *fear*, the more we fight feeling anxious, the more adrenaline we release and the more we perpetuate the cycle of panic. Similar is true of depression.** In Chapter 3 we talked about the changes that happen in the brain when we're depressed; often these changes are triggered by change or stress. In any event, studies show there are abnormally high levels of stress hormones in depressed people, along with depleted levels of dopamine, one of the 'pleasure' hormones. As with anxiety, we get caught in a cycle:

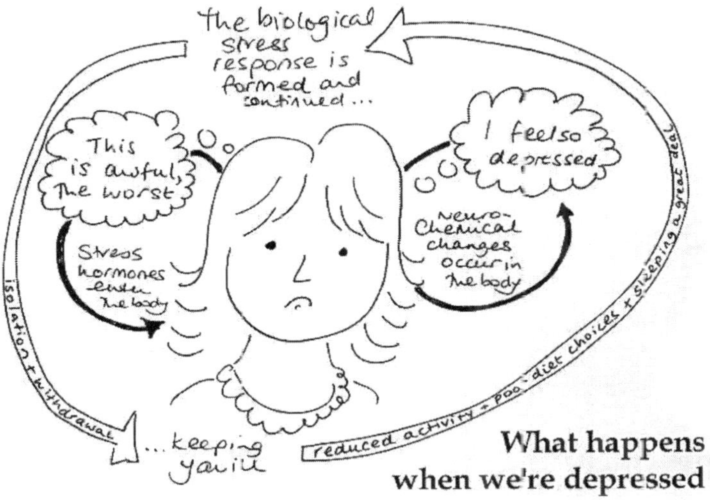

What happens when we're depressed

[25] https://www.beyondblue.org.au/the-facts

- Chemical changes make you 'feel depressed' - they lower your mood and reduce your energy levels
- These low thoughts send messages through your body which your body registers as stress
- This activates the stress response again, adding to symptoms

So on both a mental and physical level, it's fair to say that **the more we hate ourselves, the worse our depression is likely to become**. This underlines why it's so good to eat well and exercise — they can help change the cycle. But when I had my breakdown, I battled my depression for weeks on end. Often I'd wish with all my heart that I could get rid of how I was feeling; I'd shout 'get out of my head!' and beat my own forehead. But over the years that followed, I came to appreciate how I was 'doing' depression and anxiety by thinking and behaving in ways which exacerbated them. Only by making friends with these troublesome aspects of my psyche could I take control of my own recovery.

Closing down, not fighting back? Kate's perspective

When I read Sarah's description of her extreme anxiety during her breakdown, I felt immense sympathy, but not total recognition. **Depression might be common, but the experience is completely individual.** So I thought giving a different perspective might reassure you that there's no right or wrong when it comes to how you're feeling, and that it can change day by day – or even minute by minute.

I'm definitely a worrier, and I fall into damaging thinking traps at times – the 'all or nothing' thinking and 'self-blame' descriptions are very familiar. But while Sarah talks of rapid thoughts and adrenaline rushes, I've experienced the blues as a strong force, pulling me down and depleting my energy. Think of a riptide, appearing as you're swimming along quite happily, and dragging you away from the safety of the shore, from normal life, and those who love you. For me, depression felt like that – the more I fought back, the more it seemed to demonstrate it was more powerful than me. Like a swimmer being swept away, I became exhausted, unable to control what was happening to my body in spite of my own determination. And as I felt the depression overwhelm me, it seemed like a defeat. I wasn't strong enough. I was weak. *Pathetic.* I gave in... it seemed like nothing could ever be the same again.

I was wrong – things did get better again. Better than before, in some ways, **because recovery from depression does provide a chance to look at your life and see what you could change to help avoid it in future**. I talk a lot more about this in Chapter 9.

Sometimes, circumstances – or that riptide – come back. The one consolation of recognising I was feeling very down years later was the knowledge that there was the possibility of feeling better again. That rescue might be some way off, but that however much I was struggling, these feelings wouldn't last forever. I didn't have to go under completely. Instead I could accept that treading water for a while would conserve my energy, so I could get better.

Being less hard on yourself

Whatever you're personal circumstances, the main thing is not to beat yourself up for being depressed. 'Very easy to say,' you may mutter. 'Not so easy to do.' I agree – and this is why it's crucial to gain understanding of our own patterns of thinking and how they are making the pit we find ourselves in even more hellish. If we can change those ways of thinking – reduce the stress, slow the panic, diminish the self-loathing – we can help ourselves a great deal.

One way depressed people make life hard for themselves is to judge themselves more harshly than they judge others. For instance, imagine if one of your friends was sad because they'd just lost their job, or you went for a walk one day and saw a child in the park laughing as they played on the swings. Would you ever berate either of them for feeling that way? Tell your friend he or she was 'bad to feel upset', or say to the child that playing on a swing is 'nothing to be happy about'? Hopefully you wouldn't; you'd comfort your friend, say you understood, and that in time things will

probably improve. You might smile at the child on the swing, and, if you're not too down yourself, feel a little of their pleasure.

Yet **when we're depressed, we tend to beat ourselves up** for not getting better quicker. We grow angry that we've not got the energy to do more. We feel scared that we'll be this sad forever. **See how differently we treat ourselves than others?** It's as if we have a boxing match with our own psyches, smashing ourselves against the ropes when we're already bloodied and in pain. A violent metaphor maybe, but that's how cruel we can be.

Lesson 1: Noticing your thoughts

At this point I'm reminded of those irritating insurance ads starring Michael Winner, where he bumped his car into a woman's car, then said to her 'Calm down dear' when she had the temerity to get annoyed with him. I don't know about you, but I find I'm even *less* likely to calm down when someone tells me to (especially if it's said in a patronising tone) than if I'm left to calm down of my own accord. **Our reactions can't be bullied into submission**, so when I ask you to consider that you can control your thoughts, I don't want you to picture some army major-like figure, barking orders at your thoughts to get back into line. Nor is it a case of shifting our perception from seeing the same glass of water as half full instead of half empty. Instead I'm inviting you to **notice your thoughts, and become aware of their limitations**.

TRY THIS: Noticing emotions

All this sounds pretty logical, but it can still be nigh-on-impossible to grasp how to shift your own negative thought patterns. So let's see how you might begin to encourage yourself to edge a little along the spectrum of low to positive mood today. Observing your emotions can seem strange at first. If so, try this exercise a few times over several days until you grow used to it.

- Start by bringing your attention to your breath.
- Notice your breathing as you inhale and exhale, keeping it slow. Notice the sensation as your lungs expand and deflate.
- Notice how you are feeling. What word best describes that emotion? Is it happy, sad, anxious, angry, irritable…?
- Accept the emotion. We've seen how the mind is connected to the body, so it is a normal bodily reaction. Don't berate yourself for feeling this way. Simply let it move through you without resisting or encouraging it.
- It can be helpful to consider what contributed to your feeling this way. Perhaps you're irritable because you found it hard to get up today, or you're anxious because you've been signed off work. Or perhaps you don't know where the emotion comes from. **The important thing is not to judge yourself for having these feelings**. They are all OK. Any time you feel yourself engaging with these thoughts in a critical way, just notice that's what you're doing, if you can, and bring your attention back to your breathing.
- You may observe that other emotions come up too. Perhaps beneath the anger is sadness, and that might take longer to emerge. That's OK too. Just breathe and notice and be a witness to your own self-criticism.
- If you're cross or sad or anxious, **you may find it useful to give yourself a while to allow the emotion to pass through you.** Don't expect to 'get over it' straight away.

Some people call this being 'mindful' of our emotions. Others like to think of it as awareness. It doesn't really matter what we call it; the main thing is that just **observing ourselves in this way, stepping back a little, can stop – or at least slow – the cycle of negative thinking, and help us deal with intense emotion which if left unnoticed can exacerbate and prolong depression. In this way we are acting like our own good friend, saying it's OK to be sad or angry or anxious, and thus taking another step on the road to Making Peace with Depression**.

Learning to be kind

I confess I tend to go 'ew' when people talk about 'learning to love themselves': it's not very British, it sounds rather gushing. Instead I'm going to invite you to *be kinder to yourself* in the hope that won't make too many sets of toes curl. **One way we can start to be kinder to ourselves is by being more aware of our thought patterns**.

Lesson 2: Accepting criticism

We're inclined to believe we know our own minds, so you might remain cynical that you're ever going to change yours. After all, if you're anything like me and the millions of other depressed people out there, you'll have been thinking the way you do for years, possibly decades. This is a book, not a miracle cure, and it's unlikely to change your thinking overnight, so to help convince you that change *is* possible, let's examine a couple of the thought patterns depressed people are particularly prone to in more detail.

EXAMPLE

This is Kate stepping in here, to confess to my own struggles with accepting criticism. I'm a perfectionist – many of us are – and I'm very self-critical. Unfortunately, that means I don't always have a sense of perspective when people are offering what's intended to be useful feedback.

I can give you countless examples of when I've taken something far too much to heart. I've been testing out some recipes lately on neighbours and though thankfully they enjoyed most of the dishes, they weren't crazy about two of my soups: 'This one needs something extra, it's bland,' they said, 'but the other is too fiery.'

I immediately convinced myself that all my recipes were complete rubbish – even the ones they said they loved – but also felt defensive. Yet I'd asked for feedback: it would be useful in making a dish better. I know I can take things too personally, so I let it sink in overnight, then reconsidered. I went back, re-tasted, experimented.

I decided that the fiery one was purely a matter of how much you like spicy food, and it could be left as it was. But the other one did need more seasoning, and twice as much fresh thyme.

There's no clearer example of differences in opinion than taste – our genes and our food experiences mean no one likes the same thing: I saw that swiftly this time, because I'm not depressed. But when **your mood is low, it's much harder to stop a negative comment hitting home** and bringing you down.

I **try to sleep on feedback if possible**: time helps us to assess what is helpful and what is not. **Often the comment we react to the most dramatically, reflects some of the concerns or instincts we already had**, but were trying to ignore.

But we also need to recognise if criticism is unfair. People's motives are not always benevolent. When I was a young TV researcher trying to get my first news report on air, a producer made me go into a studio over and over to try to record a script and every time he was harsher about my voice: 'You sound like Minnie Mouse on helium,' was one comment I'll never forget. Of course, the tenser we are, the higher-pitched we can sound. In retrospect, I had the voice of a young woman: a little high, but clear and pleasant. In the end, another producer gave me a break, I got on air, and that was that.

The more you understand your own tendencies, the more you can filter feedback, so you take the useful information and block the negativity from people who *don't* have your interests at heart. Now back to Sarah...

TRY THIS: Imagine making a sandwich

Let me share an exercise that helped give me a useful and healthier perspective on criticism.[26] It's best done with at least one other person so next time you're with a couple of friends or family members, why don't you give it a go? You'll need to read it out loud.

1. Sit down, altogether, and each close your eyes.
2. Now, picture a loaf of bread. Imagine yourself taking that loaf, putting it on a bread board, and reaching for a knife. Cut yourself a couple of slices. Then go to the

[26] Another version of this exercise also appears in *Making Friends with Anxiety*.

fridge and get out some spread, and something nice to put in the middle, and make yourself a sandwich. (Remember to pause so you can do this too!)

3. Open your eyes. Next, ask the people you are with to describe what they imagined, each in turn.
4. They may need prompting, so get them to think of what the breadboard was like, and then the bread — was it brown or white? Crumbly or squishy? Or maybe it a baguette or made of rye… Where was the knife? In a drawer? On a magnetic strip on the wall? How about the spread — was it butter or something else? What did you each put in your sandwich?
5. Finally, it's your turn. What was your imaginary scene like?

What you'll find is that **no two people will have envisaged exactly the same situation**. One person may have used a plastic chopping board, another one made of wood. One of you may have made cucumber sandwiches cut into four small triangles, another a giant cheese and pickle doorstep.

This exercise illustrates how **we each bring our own experiences to bear on someone else's words or story.** As a writer, it helped me see that every sentence has as many different interpretations as it does readers (which goes some way to explaining how one person's 5* book is another's 1*). There's no way I can control these responses – just as Kate couldn't control the responses of her recipe tasters, and nor can you if you are criticized. To try and do so is as futile as trying to control someone's thoughts.

Understanding that criticism invariably comes from the personal perspective of the critic can be helpful distancing us from the harshness of words and lessening their impact. Obviously, this is only one example of changed thought processes, but **from small shifts like these bigger breakthroughs can come.** And perhaps next time you feel yourself bristling or fighting back tears when someone criticizes you, pause to reflect on the following:

- **People, products, places and events are rarely, if ever, *all* good or all bad**. The truth is likely to fall between the two.

Life isn't purely gloom and doom (even though it feels that way when we're depressed), nor is it all joy and celebration.

- In fact, research shows people don't trust products with 100% positive reviews, Similarly, we don't tend to respond well to those we see as 'a goody two-shoes', whereas if someone is *less* than perfect, it makes us warm to them. Think how much more interesting flawed characters are in fiction, for instance, than ones who are perfect from the off.
- Ask yourself **what's wrong with *your* taking a few missteps? Being average occasionally?** When people say 'be your own best friend', they're often encouraging us to be kinder to ourselves. Sometimes this involves lowering our standards a little.
- Finally, ask yourself if there **is an opportunity for you to learn anything from the criticism offered**, and as for the rest of the feedback, if it's of no use, picture yourself letting it go, like a balloon up into the sky…

…or, if that sounds too saccharin, simply remind yourself that **each person uses their loaf differently**.

Lesson 3: Learning to worry less

Some people have a tendency to chew things over. But whilst this approach might ease digestion, it doesn't do the same for our mental health: **ruminating about the darker side of life can fuel depression, big time.**

Many of those prone to ruminating (and I include myself in this) believe we're gaining insight from mulling over problems. Sometimes that may be true. I'm sure Franklin put in hours of study before coming up with his light bulb moment, and Einstein chewed over a few light years of physics prior to positing the theory of relativity. More often than not, however, ruminating can help fuel the cycle of despair we mentioned at the start of this chapter.

Sometimes we worry about what we've done or events that have happened, at other times we worry about what's yet to come. But we all know that **you can't change the past** (though we often forget that fact). **As for the future, it's yet to arrive,** and the majority of our worries won't become real situations anyway. Meanwhile churning issues over and over uses up a lot of energy. Wouldn't it be great to **loosen the grip these thoughts have on us, thereby freeing up our minds and lightening mood?**

One way to become less self-focused is to distract yourself, according to psychologist of Yale University Susan Nolen-Hoeksema, PhD. Her studies with Sonja Lyubomirsky, PhD, of Stanford University show that distracted ruminators recall negative events – such as being dumped by a partner – less often than non-distracted ruminators. **Distraction stops us focusing so much on our problems and blaming ourselves**.

EXAMPLE

Recently a publisher rejected a novel idea that I'd proposed. I'd spent a couple of months writing the beginning in the hopes of whetting their appetite, and was very disappointed when I read this news. The good thing is that I was away on holiday when the email came through. My husband, Tom, and I had just arrived in Rome, and Tom was eager to go sight-seeing. I told him what had happened and he gave me a hug, wiped my tears, then listened to me rant for a few minutes. Not much later, we went out to St. Peter's as planned. Result? I got over it pretty quickly, considering.

Obviously it's not always so easy to distract yourself – if you're elderly or have a chronic illness, for instance, it can be hard to find ways to occupy your mind – one reason depression is prevalent in these sectors of the population.

'But I can't just *stop* worrying!' you may say in this instance.

Try not to be impatient: learning to worry less is a gradual process. The **first step is to recognize that it's happening.** Then, if you can't distract yourself, **try to reappraise the situation, questioning your own negative perceptions of events and/or high expectations of others or yourself.**

TRY THIS: Dealing with worry

Let's see how we can put this into practice. Take something you're worried about today. Now ask:

- **Is it helpful to have this worry**? Imagine if you're poised to take an exam, for example. Is it constructive to tell yourself you're going to fail it? Is it going to help you pass, or is it more likely to make you anxious and scared and thus affect your performance?
- **Is your worry a half-formed idea?** Many worries can be lessened by being identified properly. Write it down - often bringing it into the open will lessen its hold.
- **Is what you're worrying about true?** Look at the evidence. Again, write it down and this time, consider both sides of the argument. Remind yourself that as someone with low mood you're likely to have been thinking more negatively than necessary. Perhaps you're seeing the situation in black and white, whereas in fact it's a shade of grey.

You also might like to try this suggestion from Kate.

I am a champion worrier, and I can even multi-worry, letting them build and build! But one really useful technique I use if I find I'm going through a period of ruminating too much is to **set aside Worry Time.**

- **I pick a time of day when I can devote myself to worrying**, and if something niggles or stresses me out, I add it to my Worry List.
- **Then at the designated time – say 8pm – I let myself worry in a concentrated way for 20 minutes**. That might be constructive – trying to think of ways to tackle the worry or reduce the probability of something going wrong. Often it becomes so tedious that I go off and do something better – or the postponement means when I go through the list, I realise how trivial most of it was!

This can be a good way to reduce the time spent ruminating, to try out gaining control over your own thoughts and, of course, to find solutions to the things that genuinely merit concern.

All the above involve taking a step outside yourself. **Becoming more de-centred helps us to foster a greater sense of calm and contentment. To this end, it's incredibly helpful if you can develop multiple sources of gratification and social support. If you've all your eggs in one basket, you're more at risk should your basket come a cropper.** It's why I wouldn't recommend dumping your friends whenever you get a new partner. If you make your partner the sole focus of your life, should the relationship flounder, it will hit you much harder. Or, to return to my book-rejection example: it probably hit me *less* hard because I'd another idea up my sleeve, in case the novel proposal didn't fly. The funny thing is, that second idea *did* take off: it's the book you're reading now.

5. 'E' is for Esteem – developing self respect

Did you ever play with a 'Slinky'? The coiled-up spring that can travel down a flight of stairs end-over-end as it stretches and reforms itself with the aid of gravity and its own momentum? Depression is similar. Once negative thoughts are triggered, we can find ourselves tumbling downward. Sometimes we end up hitting rock bottom, which is what we'll talk about in Chapter 7, but sometimes we can manage to stop the Slinky half way down the staircase. So let's look at another major factor in depressive thinking – low self-esteem. An awareness of this issue can help you catch yourself before you fall that far. Then we'll explore ways to improve self-esteem and lift mood.

The impact of poor self-esteem

'Poor self-esteem' and its opposite, 'good self-esteem', are phrases psychologists use a lot. What they're broadly referring to is self-worth or self-belief – the degree to which we value ourselves and our place in the world. **Self-esteem is closely linked to self-confidence. People who believe in themselves are less concerned with getting approval from others and are more able to be themselves and feel happy that way.**

The roots of self-esteem often lie in the messages received from significant people like our parents and siblings in childhood; these messages can become incorporated into belief systems resulting in thoughts such as 'I must always achieve if I'm to be considered worthwhile'. The idea of a critical inner voice is not new.

It's a similar concept to what Freud called our 'superego' and Jung the 'animus'; both thought we'd never be shot of this voice entirely, nor would we want to be, because, put simply, it keeps us in check and stops the ego running wild.

Occasional self-doubt is a normal part of life, but **when the inner critic becomes too vocal or harsh, we can end up miserable**. A traumatic event such as a divorce or redundancy can also shatter self-esteem, leading to a period of chronic or excessive self-criticism that can make us very low indeed. Often we get caught in a cycle of negative thinking and this can deepen depression.

The good news is that although poor self-esteem is linked to low mood, intervention can occur at any stage. But first let's unravel some of the ways poor self-esteem tends to reveal itself.

The cycle of poor self-esteem

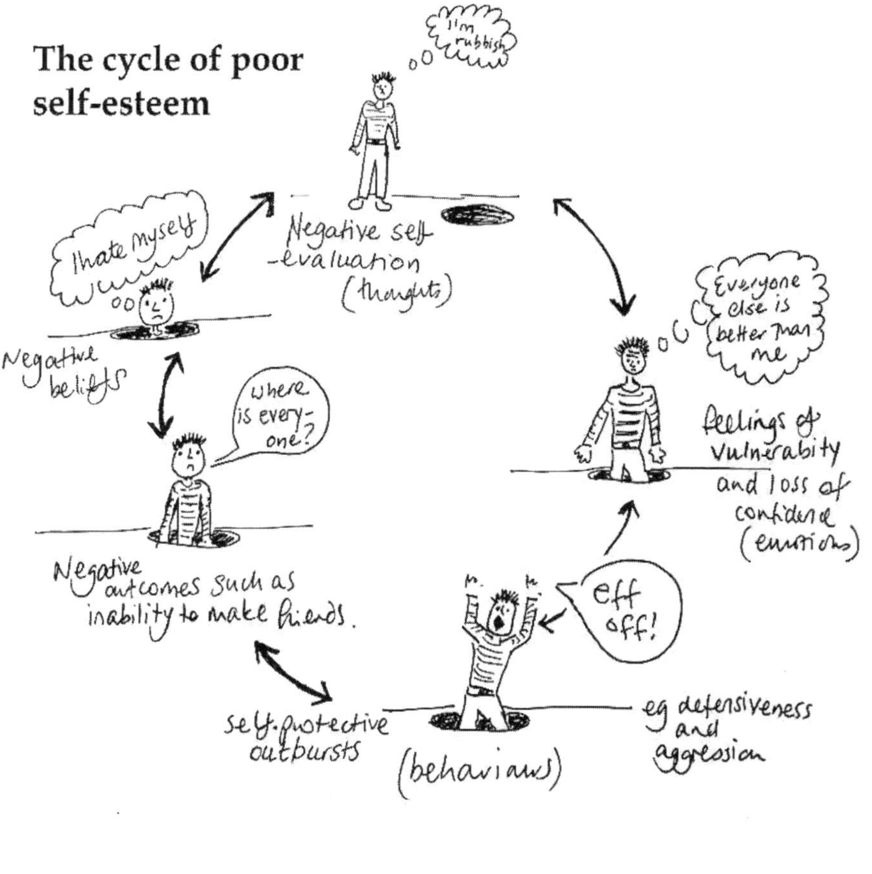

Being too nice has a price

Do you…

- Want to make everyone happy
- Dislike upsetting people
- Adapt to ease things for others
- Often ignore or devalue your own desires
- Avoid conflict because you fear negative repercussions
- Frequently take on the role of peacemaker
- Feel responsible for others' problems
- Need to be accepted?

If so, chances are you're a bit of a 'people-pleaser' – someone who is more concerned about being nice to others than to themselves. I know it's hard to imagine that being nice to others might indicate anything self-destructive, but remember I said people tend not to warm to a 'goody two shoes'? **Too much niceness can end up alienating us from others and creating an atmosphere**.

- People don't trust people who are always nice – in the same way we don't trust products with only positive reviews, it can make us feel they are 'hiding' something
- People who are always nice shy away from confrontation, so others can never be sure if they will be supported by them in a crisis situation
- Nice behaviour thus generates a sense of uncertainty and limits intimacy by placing people on their guard

More importantly in terms of depression, **being too nice to others invariably has a negative impact on the nice person themselves.** If you're one of life's overly good eggs, it means you are denying big parts of yourself. **By holding in 'bad' emotions – aggression, anger, irritation, yearning, desire, self-satisfaction and so on – the nice person is bottling up fuel for an explosion**. And when a good egg sees red, boy, do they see red! As well as being a shock for both parties, it can be much harder to recover from an intense conflict; insults are easily hurled in the heat of the moment.

We can also turn our anger inward which may lead to physical illness and, according to Freud and lots of psychotherapists since, to depression. This is the main reason it's worth working on our low self-esteem if we're trying to improve our mental health.

Passive-aggression — indirect expression of hostility

Of course people-pleasing and explosive outbursts aren't the only signs of poor self-esteem. We humans are waaay more complicated than that! **Sometimes, because it's impossible to be nice to everyone whilst at the same time being kind to ourselves, the constant denial of our own desires emerges in passive-aggression.** Passive-aggressive behaviours include

- Procrastinating — pretending not to see, hear, remember or understand requests
- Repeatedly failing to accomplish tasks you are asked to do
- Sulking, withdrawing or giving others the silent treatment
- Making excuses rather than acknowledging responsibility
- Constantly turning up late to things
- Gossiping and saying things that are resentful or bitter

We all do some of these things from time to time, but when we do them repeatedly it's not healthy for us or our relationships, because actually we're using indirect hostility to get our own needs met. Manipulating or punishing others isn't 'nice' but it stems from a similar place. But of course **unbridled selfishness is not the way forward either, and nor is aggression. If we're to keep depression at bay, far better to gain a deeper understanding of what's OK and what's not OK for us, and learn how to express these desires clearly and cleanly.**

Boundaries – a tool to help look after your mental health

We all have different boundaries — in the animal kingdom too. Take Mo, our neighbour's cat. She's boss of about 15 gardens *and* the patch of wasteland close to where we live. She's huge, beautiful and fearless, and keen to lay claim to our patio. Our cat, Thor, on the other hand, is much milder-natured, in spite of his name. He's a similar size, yet seldom ventures beyond our back wall, and when Mo comes into our garden, he tends to growl in a half-hearted way. It's only when she goes into the kitchen to steal his food that he'll fluff up, hiss and see her off his territory.

Psychologically, the borders or limits we set for ourselves in relation to others vary from one individual to another in a similar fashion: what's OK for me physically, emotionally, socially or sexually may not be OK for you. But although we're all different, it's possible to generalize: **people with healthy boundaries make good choices of who they trust and how much they trust them; people with unhealthy boundaries are vulnerable to abuse**. Those who lack self-esteem almost always have unhealthy boundaries because they find it hard to assert their needs around other people, just as Thor finds it hard to assert himself around Mo. He's the feline equivalent of a 'people pleaser', whereas Mo is so aggressive that if she were human, she would risk becoming isolated and lonely.

If you're the sort of person who often says 'yes' because it's easier, or tends to tell people what they want to hear rather than speaking the truth, chances are your boundaries are on the weak side, rather like Thor. Unhealthy boundaries can reveal themselves in a myriad of ways.

- Talking at an intimate level at first meeting
- Staying in a job we hate because we're scared to lose security
- Falling in love with people within hours of meeting them
- Acting on first sexual impulses
- Going against personal values to please others
- Touching a person without asking
- Taking the blame for other people's problems
- Allowing someone to take as much as they can from you

- Letting others direct your life
- Having trouble asking for support
- Letting others define you
- Falling apart so someone will take care of you

See how there's an overlap to over-niceness and passive-aggression? So how can we change these behaviours? Often it boils down to one thing: **people with weak boundaries find it hard to say 'no'**.

Learning to say 'no'

Many of us find it hard to say 'no' because we believe it seems petty and small-minded at best, aggressive and rude at worst. 'Yes', on the other hand, we associate with being kind, caring and selfless. But if you think about it rationally, you can't possibly say 'yes' to everything. There simply isn't time and no one has boundless energy and if we end up taking on too much as a result, we get worn out. **So to be kind to yourself and counter depression, you *have* to start setting boundaries. It's difficult to do at first as you won't be used to it, and sometimes we muddle rejection and refusal so feel guilty. Try not to feel bad about it: saying 'no' is a way of being your own best friend.**

TRY THIS: Practise saying 'no'

Next time someone asks you to do something and you feel yourself balking, say 'I'll think about it' or something similar before responding. You can say 'I need to check my diary' if you want to buy time or, if they've phoned you, you could say 'I'll call you back' . This gives you a chance to catch yourself before you automatically say 'yes'. Then, when you're ready, get back to them, and say 'no'.

- Keep it brief
- Speak slowly and with warmth
- Be honest about your feelings

This is the first step in learning to be more assertive, and it can have a knock-on effect. **By being more assertive and stating our needs, we can become more confident, and the more confident we feel the more assertive we become, and so on.** Before you know it, you'll have that Slinky defying gravity and moving back up those stairs!

'It's not me, it's you' — learning what's your 'stuff'

We've seen how negative beliefs about ourselves and situations can deepen low mood. But **sometimes we can pick up on other people's negativity** and this can have an impact on our state of mind too. **Having strong boundaries can help protect us against getting too drawn in to other people's 'stuff'.**

EXAMPLE

Let me illustrate by telling you about Sylvia. A while ago Sylvia felt a lump in her lower abdomen. She went to the doctor, and was advised she had a malignant tumour in her uterus and needed to have a hysterectomy. The surgeon said he couldn't be sure if she'd need chemotherapy until he'd got the results after the operation.

Sylvia is an optimistic woman on the whole, but she had to wait several weeks for the op, and a fortnight after that for the results, and during this time she was very anxious. Fortunately she has loving kids and lots of friends who rallied round. The one person who was not so supportive was her husband, Greg. He's usually a decent bloke, but on this occasion he told Sylvia there was 'no point discussing' her worries, although she found that voicing her fears helped her feel better. He closed down dialogue, so she felt she was treading on eggshells around him. For two months Greg continued to behave badly. He didn't even drive her to the hospital to get the results, such was the extent that he refused to get involved.

Fortunately the surgeon gave Sylvia good news; the operation was all the treatment she needed. When she'd taken stock, Sylvia tried to talk to Greg and suggested they go to counselling, but he didn't want to. Gradually their relationship has got back on an even keel, and now she says it's as if 'nothing ever happened'.

I share this not to illustrate how men can be pigs and women towers of strength (because although they sometimes can, the reverse is also true) but because it's a good example of a thinking error on Greg's part. Instead of facing his fears and managing his upset so he could support his wife, he went into denial and his reactions became skewed. In circumstances like these it would have been easy for Sylvia to have thought the problems were the result of something *she'd* done and that it was her fault.

Sylvia shed many tears during those awful weeks and had moments of awful self-doubt. But mostly she got angry – a healthy reaction given Greg's behaviour, but someone who had a less clear sense of herself could have been severely affected. Next time you feel yourself being drawn into someone else's issues, it's worth thinking of Sylvia and trying to channel a similar sense of your autonomy.

TIP: If your low mood is being affected by another person, remember that to alter your mood you need to focus on yourself. Are you caring for yourself physically? Watch your stress levels, take time to be with friends, get enough sleep. If your relationship is draining you more than it is sustaining you, consider ending it.

It's very easy to get caught up in other people's issues, as I learned to my cost when living with an alcoholic boyfriend many years ago. I found myself drawn into his warped thinking and self-destruction, and nearly went under completely along with him. Luckily, I extricated myself from the relationship in the nick of time, and once I was out, I was able to see what had been going on. Nonetheless **this is no laughing matter – abusive and violent relationships can easily develop when we feel too personally responsible for other people's wellbeing**. No one lives in a vacuum, nor would we want to, but unless we're very resilient, we can end up being manipulated and horribly compromised, and if we're anxious or depressed it can be especially hard to see what's going on as our thoughts tend to be muddled anyway.

When we're vulnerable and have poor self-esteem, unhealthy relationship dynamics can provide fertile ground for low mood to take hold, and it may be hard to unravel on your own what's causing what. Family members, colleagues and even friends can damage us too. **If you think a toxic relationship is seriously impacting your mental health, I'd urge you to seek support from outside sources such as** www.al-anonuk.org.uk **or www.nationaldomesticviolencehelpline.org.uk in the UK or www.loveisrespect.org in the US, and to consider counselling and/or therapy to help you find a way through**. It's what your best friend would advise, so be a best friend to yourself.

6. 'S' is for 'Safety Behaviours' — understanding and improving the ways we cope with stress

In the last few chapters we've been looking at the specific patterns of thinking which are associated with depression, and seen how we get caught in a cycle of negativity. **There's another way we may unwittingly fuel depression too — and that's with our *behaviour*.**

A behaviour is a conscious or subconscious response to some sort of stimulation or impetus in the mind and/or body. If you hurt yourself by, say, stubbing your toe, you might flinch and say 'ow!', or if you feel sad or upset, you might get tearful. Flinching, saying 'ow!' and crying are behaviours — ways we act or conduct ourselves as a result of a particular situation.

Behaviours, thoughts and feelings are all linked, like this:

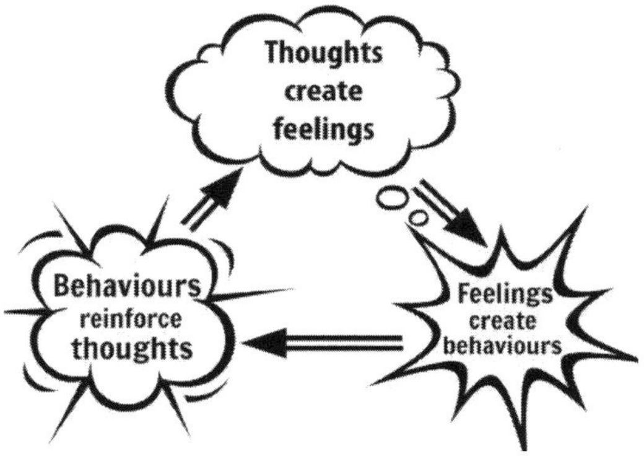

When we are low, certain behaviours are more common. We're more likely to get tearful, for example, withdraw socially or not eat or sleep much. Many of these are not a concern in themselves. Crying can be a great release and it's not *that* hard to survive a few nights of bad sleep.

Coping mechanisms

These sorts of behaviours are often referred to by psychiatrists as 'coping mechanisms' or 'safety behaviours' and they stem from the same, primitive part of the brain as the fight or flight instinct (see page 54). We all have coping mechanisms to some degree, and, as with fear and anxiety, to an extent we need them. It's natural to try and stay safe, plus it's a vital element of being kind to ourselves.

The trouble comes when behaviours become prolonged or frequent so that we end up stuck in certain modes of being. Opting out of going for a jog because it's raining is OK, but if you rarely venture outdoors then soon it becomes a habit, as the more you repeat it, the more entrenched the behaviour can become. Self-medicating is another coping mechanism, so if you have to get totally hammered in order to engage socially, you can probably see rationally that it's not helping you cope or feel safe, but still, part of you believes it is. Examples of safety behaviours include:

- **Being reckless** – gambling, going on wild shopping sprees
- **Socially isolating** – hiding under the duvet, refusing to leave the house, rejecting others before they reject you
- **Suffering in silence** – not expressing feelings is both a cause and symptom of depression
- **Not exercising** – you don't have the energy and you don't think it'll do any good
- **Running away** – cancelling appointments, avoiding situations and events
- **Not responding** – ignoring the phone and emails, not opening your post
- **Seeking reassurance** – always pleasing others in case they don't like what you do
- **Immersing yourself** – in work, caring for others
- **Procrastinating** – putting things off
- **Not washing** – either yourself or keeping your home clean
- **Overeating** – to comfort yourself with a 'consolation prize'
- **Not eating enough**
- **Creating diversions** – generating alternative problems or focusing on someone else
- **Obsessively ruminating** – going over and over problems
- **Handing over** – asking someone else to rescue you
- **Self-medicating** – with alcohol or drugs

...and so on. These tactics can offer short-term relief, but in the long run often make our mental health worse. Broadly speaking there are three main ways these behaviours have a negative impact:

- We **avoid** responsibilities and situations
- They are **self-destructive**
- They **lower mood** even more

Often they do all three.

Avoidance

People with depression often develop avoidance behaviours such as procrastinating and ruminating. **Once we start to avoid, the process of generalization[27] takes place and we end up avoiding more and more situations**. What was once staying at home to look after yourself and not get rained upon if it's horrid outside can evolve into a fear of leaving the house, which in turn means you become increasingly isolated, unfit and lacking in energy. Eventually you may end up with agoraphobia, so what was once helping you to cope becomes a problem in itself.

[27] Generalization: The transfer of a learned response from one stimulus to a similar stimulus.

The trouble is, the longer we put off facing our fears, the more worrying things we are frightened of become. **Avoiding a situation, not once but continually, means we never learn if we can manage it. This can erode self-confidence and deepen depression.**

Self-destructiveness

At first the idea that self-destruction could be a 'safety behaviour' might seem nonsensical. 'Surely a harmful behaviour can't ever *help* someone cope,' you might say. Yet according to psychologist Pamela Cantor[28], there is a strong relationship between depression and high-risk behaviours. **Excessive drinking, drug abuse, unsafe sex and cutting are all self-injurious behaviours that individuals may use to provide temporary relief from intense emotional pain**, she explains. Often the person 'has a void inside'; they may feel so much pain from the past that they end up harming themselves instead of helping themselves, says clinical psychologist Cara Gardenswartz.

These coping mechanisms offer little reprieve, however. Whilst alcohol or smoking weed might relax you initially, for example, they are both depressants so will not lift your mood longer term, and they can also interact negatively with prescribed medications. What's more, if used excessively, these behaviours are very dangerous. The physical impact is obvious: liver damage from alcoholism, sexually transmitted diseases from unprotected sex, infections and scarring from cutting one's skin.

Yet we've nearly all used some of these methods to help cope with stress to a greater or lesser degree: who can honestly say they've *never* got drunk in the wake of bad news, or eaten a whole box of chocolates or too much cake to cheer themselves up after a tough week at work? Not me (or Kate or Patrick), that's for sure.

TIP: Try to recognise when you're drinking or comfort eating to avoid being in touch with feelings. Alcohol or comfort foods should be a treat, not a treatment.

Whilst many of us are aware that constructive action rather than a retreat into substance use is far more likely to help lift

---

[28] http://www.webmd.com/depression/features/depression-and-risky-behavior#

depression in the long run, the prospect of eliminating alcohol and drugs completely can be daunting. Remember that whilst using none is ideal (particularly in the case of recreational drugs), reducing your intake is better than becoming overwhelmed and ending up back where you were. Equally, alcohol in moderation is preferable to binge drinking.

We'll return to the subject of self-destructive behaviour in Chapter 7, but whatever form avoidance takes - drinking, taking drugs, over-eating, not eating enough, staying in bed, fleeing — the effect is the same: we create a vicious circle where we're trapped by our own behaviour. **Thus 'safety behaviours' can end up constraining us too, which is why it's crucial to address them if we're to improve our mental health.**

The vicious circle

Remember we talked about how the mind and body are linked in Chapter 3? In fact we can add a *fourth* element into the cycle along with thoughts, feelings and behaviours — our *physical reactions* or symptoms. Let me illustrate.

EXAMPLE 1

Pete's boss, Mr Mears, was always blaming Pete for everything, including issues that weren't his responsibility. Pete thought Mr Mears was being unfair, but still he couldn't help take it personally, and when his boss snapped one day and fired him, Pete was devastated. He went home and started drinking, and when he woke up with a hangover, he felt even worse. He couldn't face seeing his mates so when they invited him out, he feigned sickness and hid under the duvet. Over the next few weeks, nothing seemed to shift his low mood. Eventually Pete was diagnosed with clinical depression.

'Poor Pete,' you may think, and you're right. Having a boss who has it in for you is no fun at all. But it's not *just* having a nasty boss that brought on Pete's depression, it's ***how he reacted to the*** emotions and these emotions affect how we behave. Our behaviour then leads to physical symptoms, and so it goes on… and on.

The vicious circle

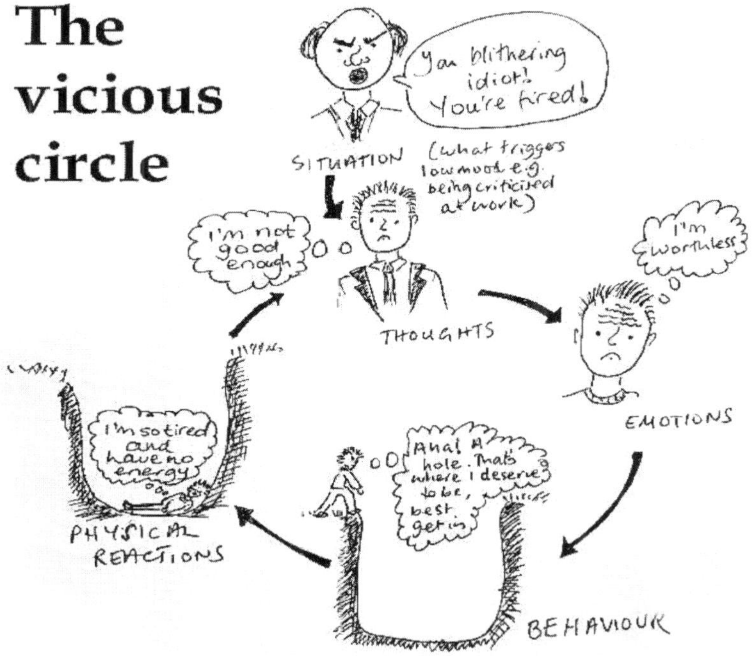

But supposing Pete was more able to distance himself from his boss's actions? Maybe he'd seen Mr Mears fire people unfairly before. Or maybe he had better self-esteem, so although losing his

Breaking the vicious circle

job still had an impact, Pete recognized it wasn't him, but Mr Mears who had the issues (just as Sylvia realized in Chapter 5). As a result, once he'd got over the shock, Pete didn't beat himself up so much, and soon saw he was better off not working for Mr Mears. Unlike depressed Pete, he gritted his teeth and set about finding another job. His *behaviour* was different: he looked through vacancies, he picked up the phone. And you don't need to be Freud reincarnated to see how this more positive way of behaving might have a knock-on effect in terms of his energy levels and mood, so Pete could avoid being caught in a vicious circle and move on.

EXAMPLE 2

I'm not blaming Pete for getting down though – and I don't want you to think I'm *blaming* you. I've a tendency to react similarly.

In the past when I've felt anxiety rising and/or my mood dropping, my reaction has always been to go to bed, and after a week or so, I'd feel absolutely vile. My head would be a whirl of negativity, I'd be consumed by self-loathing and self-criticism. When I wasn't panicky, I was exhausted. I really think people who make light of either anxiety or depression haven't experienced either on the same level as those of us who suffer badly, and if you're feeling in any way similar now, you have my heartfelt sympathy.

Gradually, however, I came to understand that I wasn't helping myself. **Depression may make us default to behaviours that aren't helpful but feel familiar**. But when I learned that my physical symptoms were largely attributable to adrenaline (again, see page 54) and thus perfectly normal, I began to realize that staying in bed, far from keeping me safe, only allowed the adrenaline to keep churning round my body with nowhere particular to go. When I realized that the behaviours I thought were helping me feel better were, in fact, making me feel worse – and not just worse mentally, *but physically too* – I was tempted to stand up and yell 'Bingo!', I felt something so crucial had clicked into place.

TIP: The first step towards changing unhelpful coping mechanisms is to recognize that you're using them *at the time you're doing it.*

Back in Chapter 3, I mentioned how helpful physical exercise can be in 'using up' adrenaline, but I also pointed out that **it's a good idea to take it slowly**. Thus, in this situation it wouldn't have been wise to jump straight out of bed and attempt a marathon. After weeks of inertia, my body wouldn't have known what had hit it, so to speak. (Not that I could run a marathon anyway, but you get my drift.) Instead, I got up and did some gentle yoga – very basic stretching and breathing. This highlights how **treatment of depression is often most effective when it takes the body into account**. It also illustrates why **it's important to be kind to yourself**.

If I'd *not* been made aware of how destructive my thought processes tended to be, and that I could change them, I might have ordered myself 'Get up! Run 26 miles!' or similar. But – forgive me if this sounds sappy – I was learning to be a better friend to myself.

Breaking the vicious circle

These two examples help to illustrate that **often it's easiest to break the vicious circle of depression not by changing one's *thoughts*, but by changing one's *behaviour***. The behaviour element of the depressive cycle is a crucial opportunity for intervention[29]– but because you're learning to be your own best friend, you can intervene *yourself*. Thus Pete intervened by changing his behaviour and actively job seeking. I intervened by getting out of bed and

[29] *Intervention* comes from the Latin *intervenire*, meaning "to come between, interrupt." When used in the context of addiction and mental health, an intervention is intended to make things better. One common use of the word refers to a specific type of meeting that happens with the family and friends of a drug addict; they join together to try to convince the drug user to change their ways and live a healthier life.

doing a little gentle exercise. For both of us, this resulted in a change to our patterns of thinking, which caused low mood to lift a little, and physical symptoms to ease. At the start it was hard but, because they're all connected, one led to another. From one small shift, bigger breakthroughs can come, as I said already.[30]

TIP: To a certain extent depression is something we *do*, and we can feel different by doing different, i.e. changing our behaviour.

There's another thing – these examples demonstrate that **tackling our fears *gradually* is more effective**. Supposing I *had* tried to run a marathon; it's easy to see how that tactic would probably have landed me right back where I'd started: in bed, heart palpitating, feeling sick and shaky. My thoughts would have been negative — 'I can't do it' — my feelings self-critical — 'I'm useless' — and so on.

Here the phrase 'learn to walk before you run' is apt. If **we start slowly, then step by step, we can build our confidence and stop avoiding everything or using such self-destructive coping mechanisms.** Sometimes this technique is called '**graded exposure**', and whether we're suffering from depression, anxiety, a phobia or panic attacks, the same approach can work well for them all. It's like taking stepping stones across a treacherous river, rather than diving straight in and hoping you can swim in a fast-flowing current.

TRY THIS: Stepping stones

Take something that you have been avoiding. Supposing you've been off work for a while, for instance, or haven't been out of the house for ages. In the case of them both the same applies:

- **Start small** – begin with the easiest situation and practise it
- **Build up gradually** – if something is too hard, look at breaking it down into smaller, more manageable chunks
- **Be kind to yourself** – pat yourself on the back for each step

[30] See page 62.

- **Don't focus on how far you've got to go** or berate yourself for not getting there immediately
- **Stop before you have reached your ultimate goal**
- **Repeat** at least once a day, each time encouraging yourself to go a little further down the path.

TIP: Set yourself small, manageable targets and reward yourself when you reach them. This can be much more effective than trying to reach one big goal. It'll make the process more enjoyable, too, because recovery from depression, like much of life, is (to coin a cliché) not all about the destination; it's about the journey.

Triggers

If we examine our depression more closely, we can sometimes find it is set off by a past experience, so **when something happens to us in the present that echoes this situation, we feel the way we felt the first time all over again. This is sometimes called 'being triggered',** and is as different for each of us as our fingerprints, as no two people have the same personal history.

Should we get triggered in some way, we can be especially susceptible to retreat into familiar ways of coping. You might avoid going on dates for a long while because your last relationship ended badly, or if you grew up in a violent and neglectful home you may turn to drinking to bury the feelings of rage and poor self-esteem.

When you come to facing a fear after you' ve been triggered, breaking the situation down into smaller, less intimidating stages can be very helpful, as we've shown. Thus if you've had a bad break-up, you could start by getting in touch with friends and family and setting yourself a regular, manageable target – aim to see a friend or family member at least twice a week… and so on. This will stop the cycle of negativity and should help to lift your mood.

But before we move on, **a few words of caution: I can't unravel what's triggering you personally**. I don't know your history, and I am not a therapist, and neither is Kate or Patrick. For us to suggest it's possible to ease deeper issues in a one-size-fits-all book would be naïve and irresponsible, and **if you find you're being repeatedly triggered and it's seriously affecting your life, we'd recommend seeking professional help**. It's here that psychotherapy, which tends to look into past experience more than the cognitive/behavioural approaches we've drawn upon thus far, can be illuminating. Part of the work of therapy is to find out what your triggers are, and a therapist can talk with you to find out more about the nature of your depression and together you can explore connections to your past. A lot of safety behaviours stem from having experienced trauma, either witnessing it or experiencing it personally, explains psychologist Mary Carole Curran.[31] She argues that all this pent-up energy often comes out in depression and risky behaviours, and says it's important to find it where it's coming from. Dealing directly with the trauma can help. I've already mentioned The British Psychotherapy Foundation, and there are further contacts at the end of this book.

In spite of all these insights, there may be times, however, when all the advice you're given barely seems to touch the sides, when neither CBT nor psychotherapy seem to help, when medication doesn't appear to be working. This is when you can find yourself hitting rock bottom, and that's what we'll look at next.

---

[31] http://www.webmd.com/depression/features/depression-and-risky-behavior#1

7. 'S' is for Suffering – reaching out if you hit rock bottom

Depression is usually self-destructive. Although there are depressed people who get into fights and emotionally abuse others, it's more usually a passive form of self-destruction; when we're depressed we tend to isolate ourselves, giving up hope and expecting the worst. We may turn to alcohol for comfort, but the glass is invariably half empty; good experiences feel temporary and unreliable, bad experiences permanent and pervasive; other people are more attractive, more successful… And whilst we may know what we ought to do to feel better, we are too depressed to do it, so we blame ourselves for lacking willpower, and this compounds our low self-esteem and self-loathing.

The pit of despair

These are the hardest and most precarious times for sufferers, when mood can slip so low that advice becomes mere noise, warns Patrick, who over the years has seen many patients feeling like this in his work as a GP. Calls go unanswered, daylight isn't welcomed. You stay in bed for hours, perhaps all day; stare into the fridge and make a plateful of food even though you're not hungry, or just shut it again feeling no appetite at all. Television is unwatchable. Work and friends are remote concepts, way beyond the curtained window.

When you're in this pit of despair, **self-mutilation and anorexia/bulimia are common.** Perhaps a little nick with a razor may restore feeling. Starving yourself may lend a sense of control. For some of us, no matter what we do, life itself feels unbearable, and we would like to ease into an absence, oblivion... So our depression may be accompanied by non-fatal suicide attempts and suicidal gestures. Impulses like driving into a wall or stepping off a high place can come out of nowhere and convince us we are going completely crazy.

All these behaviours are very common with severe depression, and suicide is often a real risk, says Patrick. Yet strangely, when you're in the middle of it, you may not even recognize that things have got this bad. Someone close may be worrying, and you might just wish they would go away. But they are all warning signs. Remember the PHQ9 test we looked at in Chapter 1? If you're feeling like this, then try testing yourself here: http://patient.info/doctor/patient-health-questionnaire-phq-9. If you're scoring higher than usual, or over 20, something is wrong. You need help. Ask for it, please.

If you're not sure how to reach out, start here: <u>help is letting people know</u>. Tell your friend, tell your loved one. People want to help when they see you like this, but often they don't know how. So give them this book and ask them to read page 91, then they should feel more able to support you. **Alternatively, tell your doctor, or talk to the Samaritans on Freephone 116 123.**[32]

Suicidal thoughts

'I remember when I first thought that my not being here anymore would make every single person around me better off. It sounds stupid, but when you feel down, you think you're only having a negative impact on people. More importantly, you feel like you make no difference to the world and that there isn't a single person who would miss you. This is when the loneliness overcomes you, and it feels like there is only one way out – to end the train of thought altogether by ending yourself.' **Sam**

[32] For worldwide suicide hotlines please visit http://www.suicide.org/international-suicide-hotlines.html

'Death must be so beautiful. To lie in the soft brown earth, with the grasses waving above one's head, and listen to silence. To have no yesterday, and no tomorrow. To forget time, to forget life, to be at peace.' **Oscar Wilde**

A final end to the woes life throws at us can seem like a solution, Patrick explains. Usually this thought is fleeting, or makes us smile or cry, and with that release it passes. However, the thought of death can continue, turning over and over again in your mind that life is no longer liveable. All pleasure is gone. All hope is gone. An ending is needed, the story of our life has to stop.

Something has gone drastically wrong. We are built, like any animal, with strong feelings of self-preservation. Nonetheless we take huge risks with our lives, willingly and happily, to the point it seems daft at times. Flying in aeroplanes, swimming in the wild sea, walking out of the front door, always assuming everything will be alright. And it usually is. But when we feel that preservation has eroded, that we are no longer worth keeping alive, then the protective mechanisms are failing.

'The thought of suicide is a great consolation: by means of it one gets through many a dark night.' **Friedrich Nietzsche**

Suicide as a thought may be a solace, as German philosopher Nietzsche suggested, but the reality is deeply troubling: over 6000 people killed themselves in the UK in 2014. Of these, the biggest group were middle-aged men.[33] They are often the people who don't seek help; they don't see their doctor, they don't tell their friends. And female suicide is on the rise.[34] It is beyond the scope of this chapter to explore why this is happening, but if you're interested, the Samaritans figures are here: http://www.samaritans.org/about-us/our-research/facts-and-figures-about-suicide and there are further references at the end of this book. Right now, more important than statistics is your welfare. **Overleaf are questions to ask yourself.**

[33] In 2013 there were 6,233 suicides recorded in the UK for people aged 15 and older. Of these, 78% were male and 22% were female. https://www.mentalhealth.org.uk/publications/fundamental-facts-about-mental-health-2015

[34] http://www.theweek.co.uk/76949/womens-suicide-rates-on-the-rise

- Do you **feel hopeless**?
- Are you becoming **more withdrawn**?
- Are you spending **more time alone**, avoiding work/friends?
- Are you in debt?
- Are you **drinking too much** alcohol, or **taking street drugs**?
- Are you already on medication, but it doesn't seem to be working?
- Has **someone close to you died**? Bereavement is a strong trigger for these feelings.

All of the above indicate your **mood is worsening**. Help is needed in the ways discussed on page 88.

Do you have a plan to end your life? Pills, a leap, a crash? **Plans are a very worrying sign. Going beyond the idea of suicide, and turning it into an actuality is a huge step.** This is the time to seek **URGENT** help. Please let your friends or medical team know. Even though things feel hopeless, **there is going to be a way forward that you haven't considered**. You're not able to think clearly. It may be like being in a dark locked room with no key to the door, no way out – someone outside the room could help you open the door. **Ask for help. Call for help. Don't wait.**

Lastly, I can't offer enough consolation. The pains and aches of life can be overwhelming. I hope some of the above has helped to guide and give clearer understanding of a stigmatised and complex situation. Sarah, Kate and I want you to stay with us, and **trust that recovery is possible.**

Self-harm

'Self-harm is something that makes absolutely no sense to someone that has never done it, but I self-harm almost all the time in some way or another – mainly by scratching and digging my fingernails into myself although I have at times cut myself. When that happened I felt totally out of control of my feelings and desperate for some way to control them. It helped to release the pressure better than anything else, and at times even just looking at the cuts seemed to help.' **Jay**

Cutting, thumping, bruising, biting, burning – if you've never deliberately hurt yourself, it is common not to understand why others choose to do so, but it's impossible to know what someone else has been through to lead them to this expression of internal pains or conflicts. All these behaviours can start early in life as coping mechanisms – children may hurt themselves and this can carry on into adulthood.

'I have unfortunately done more than consider self-harm. Self-harm is a very personal thing and everyone has their own reasoning and feelings behind it. Me, I feel like I deserve the pain. I feel like this is my punishment for every time I screw up. That it is some form of conversion to become a better person. That pain will deter me from messing up again.' **Eva**

Here's Patrick again with a steer.

Watch out for an increase in the frequency and severity of self-harm, as this tends to suggest that things are unstable. Once again, please ask for help. If you're on your own in this situation, do go to A&E and speak to their liaison psychiatry team. The chain of action is thus:

Increasing injury → alert people close to you → see your GP → attend A&E

If you've had a negative experience in one A&E, try another.

You can access the NICE guidance on the management and treatment of self-harm by medical staff here: www.nice.org.uk/guidance/cg16. There are further resources at the end of the book.

It is important to clarify that self-harm is not an indicator that someone wants to end their life. Yet suicidal thoughts can accompany it, and if these start emerging then a different strategy is needed, as we discussed on page 88.

Igniting hope

Without things to look forward to, hope is difficult to ignite, so here's an exercise I use in my care of patients with terminal illnesses. **We focus on goals; you can do the same in these tough times.** Pick your moment. Not a time of crisis; but when things are less fraught.

TRY THIS: Lighting dark days

- *What can you look forward to today?* A treat. A small thing. A nice warm bath alone, or whilst your friend sits with you.
- *What can you plan for the week ahead?* A treat. A simple thing. A stroll in the park. A trip to see someone close to you for a cup of tea.
- *What can you plan for the month ahead?* A treat. A simple thing. A coffee with a friend in a local café. An hour in the quiet of an art gallery or library. A trip to the cinema. What do you really fancy doing? A break from your routine.

- *What can you plan for the months ahead?* Is there a birthday or an anniversary? What would you like to do to mark that event? What would you like to wear? Is there a holiday to plan? A weekend away with friends?
- *And now something fanciful.* What would please you? An imaginary thing. A different job? A new love? Painting the lounge walls bright pink or silver? A flight to Greece, a sunny beach? Meeting your favourite singer or writer? There's no end to this list. Imagination is such a marvellous thing, and one of the first sensations to disappear when depression arrives.

Helping someone in despair – tips for your nearest and dearest

Blinded by feelings of self-loathing and hopelessness, a suicidal person can't see any way of finding relief except through death. But despite their desire for the pain to stop, most suicidal people are deeply conflicted about ending their own lives. They wish there was an alternative to suicide, but they just can't see one.

Patrick says: If you have a friend or family member who is suicidal or self-harming it can be frustrating, but my advice is that the greatest help is physical presence, just being there. In my consultations I try to offer a calm, quiet space for thoughts to come to the surface. I don't interrupt, I don't offer suggestions, I let my patients talk. This tends to encourage people to open up. The more they talk, the more the risk is hopefully reduced or defused.

- **Do not, under any circumstances, leave your suicidal friend alone, and remove drugs and sharp objects.**
- **Finding out about suicidal thoughts or a desire to self-harm does not put those thoughts into people's heads, so establishing if they have a specific plan is important**. In order to do this, **your priority is to listen and pay attention.**
- **Show you are listening** by looking, nodding, repeating back what you've heard. Acknowledgement is key.
- **Don't offer advice. Don't try to fix what you don't know is broken.** The important thing for desperate and suicidal people to understand is that the feelings pass, but saying this is often not as helpful as just being there until the impulse subsides. Instead just listen.
- **Offer your hand to hold. Offer a drink of something warm.**
- **When your friend has tired of talking and things are clearer, focus on getting them proper mental health treatment. Think of where you can get help.** Is it from someone in the family, someone close by? Is it from a spiritual source like a priest, rabbi, imam? Perhaps talk to the Samaritans, and encourage your friend to do this too. Be with them. Be present.
- **Will your friend come to see their doctor with you? Will they go to A&E?** If there is a crisis, then A&E usually have a

liaison psychiatry team member present who is there to help. Not an ideal place, busy and chaotic, but help is there. If your friend is able to wait, A&E may be a bit quieter in the morning when things are less hectic.

- **Lastly, if you are worried about your friend and you fear they will hurt themselves, call 999.** The police can track people, and ambulance crews can take patients to hospital for self-poisoning, for psychiatric assessment, and for safety.

Remember, **your goal isn't to talk them out of their plan; it is to engage them and get them involved so that they can get the treatment that they need.** Ways forward will emerge.

Looking after yourself while you support someone else

These are tough times, the hardest. **If you are looking after someone who feels this bad, who is looking after you?** This crisis will hopefully pass, but another may arise. And if it does, you may have to do it all again.

Please remember that it is not your fault your friend or family member is depressed – I know this can be hard if your relationship is a close one but you really are not responsible for anyone else's mental illness. Once your friend or family member is safe, it often helps to give yourself space, and ask for support when you need it.[35] It's a good idea to compile your own support list with details of organisations and people to contact, and to keep it handy. There is also a detailed free guide on supporting someone is who suicidal available for download from Mind.[36]

[35] Carers UK helpline: 0808 808 7777 carersuk.org for information on caring.
[36] Find the PDF here: http://www.mind.org.uk/information-support/types-of-mental-health-problems/suicide-supporting-someone-else/#.V_fwgeArKhc

8. 'I' is for Imagination — creativity and depression

Recovering from depression is not like healing from an injury. If you were to break a leg, your doctor could tell you - at least roughly - how long you will be in plaster. Depression isn't like that; each person's recovery is different.

Coming through the other side

If you've been depressed for a while, it may be hard to remember what feeling 'normal' was like, which can make it difficult to gauge how far you've come. When you're in intense emotional distress, it can be agony waiting for medication to have an effect, and it often takes time to connect with a new therapist or counsellor, too. There's ample research to show that treatment for depression *does* work[37], so please stick with it. Nonetheless **it's important to know that you are not alone**, and it's here that music, poetry, prose, paintings and sculpture can break through barriers and reveal an emotional truth in such a raw and relatable way that they reach out to us in our in pain.

For some it's the powerful language of literature that cuts through the depression and self-loathing. For others it might be a song lyric that can pierce the noise and hurt, or a particular painting that shows us others have suffered as we do. And just as reading, listening and looking at others' work can bring relief and solace, so can being actively creative.

---

[37] www.dbsalliance.org/site/PageServer?pagename=education_statistics_depression and www.nimh.nih.gov/news/science-news/2009/long-term-depression-treatment-leads-to-sustained-recovery-for-most-teens.shtml

Writing as therapy

Kate writes: **Many people find the process of writing can be cathartic** – the word comes from the Greek 'cleansing, purgative' and means *providing psychological relief through the open expression of strong emotions.*

Whilst we may talk about 'pouring our heart out' to someone else, when we're feeling ashamed or guilty about our emotions, it can be much easier to express them on paper, without ever intending to share them. Diary-writing is the most obvious example: for centuries, young and old have used a journal as a confidante, telling secrets and unravelling problems in a 'safe space'. (Though my own teenage diary has much more about how cold it was at netball and how annoying my Geography teacher was.) A more structured approach can bring real benefits: studies suggest that embarking on a short programme of self-guided expressive writing can result in fewer stress-related visits to the doctor,[38] improved immune function and blood pressure results, less absenteeism, and raised mood.

Secret words, public stories

Creative writing of stories, poems or memoir is often seen as something we do in order to share, but **writing as therapy is a dialogue with yourself** via the blank page. At times, the words or ideas you're expressing might lead to something you *want* to make public – but **it's really important to give yourself the freedom to write without the emotional risk of being read by anyone**. You don't want to censor yourself.

I've written for a living in different forms since I started work: first as a journalist/TV reporter, and more recently as a novelist and non-fiction author. My natural instinct is therefore to frame things as 'stories' that other people might enjoy reading or listening to. But when I want to sort something out in my own mind – both when I have been feeling low, and also just when I want a clearer picture of things – I take out a notepad and pen, and begin to write. Sometimes it's 'Morning Pages'[39] – filling several sheets with uncensored thoughts as they come, as soon as I get up. More often, I might write, diary-style, about something troubling me. Sometimes I doodle or draw as well: because I know no one will see it, or judge, I can

---

38 Emotional and physical health benefits of expressive writing, Karen A Baikie, Kay Wilhelm Advances in Psychiatric Treatment Aug 2005, http://apt.rcpsych.org/content/11/5/338

39 The idea for Morning Pages originates from *The Artists' Way: A Spiritual Path to Higher Creativity* by Julia Cameron. The book is designed for people wanting to lead a more creative life and has numerous therapeutic exercises.

do exactly what I want. I have even written poetry – quite self-indulgent poetry, I confess – but again, because it's not something I ever plan to share, that doesn't matter!

Ad hoc writing can be useful at any point. But the most thorough studies have been conducted using a structured, but simple, schedule of writing every day for a week about things that are troubling you. It's a technique pioneered by Dr James Pennebaker, former Chair of Psychology at the University of Texas. His theory is that if we've buried traumas in our past, then it stresses the body physically and mentally – and allowing those feelings to come out through writing can reduce that stress. His work has been repeated hundreds of times all over the world, with similar results.

TRY THIS: Write away

Expressive writing is simple. It involves writing about your feelings for 15-20 minutes, for four consecutive days. Please note: **if you are very low at the moment, do talk to your doctor or therapist before trying this**. Short-term, writing about things that upset you can be distressing: though studies show this isn't usually harmful long-term.

- Set aside a time to write: Dr Pennebaker suggests at the end of the working day, or before bed. Make sure you don't have to rush off afterwards, so you have time to compose yourself.
- Set an alarm on your phone or clock for 15-20 minutes.

- You can use a pen, paper, computer, or even dictate into a recorder if you don't feel like writing it down.
- Don't worry about grammar and spelling: they don't matter here.

It's up to you what you write about – remember, no one else will ever see it. You could consider:

- Whatever is worrying you right now – difficult decisions, dreams, struggles in relationships or with addictions.
- Difficult experiences in the past – especially anything you've been avoiding thinking about or talking about.

- Anything else you feel might be affecting you in an unhealthy way.
- You can write about the same subject each day or different topics.
- If you find yourself writing about the same thing – or even repeating the same words – again, it's not a problem.
- You may feel upset or want to cry as you write, or afterwards. But in the studies, people felt better after a couple of hours.
- Recognise your own limits: if you find you're getting too upset, switch to something else. You don't have to push yourself further than you feel able to go.
- If you feel very overwhelmed, you can stop. It's in your hands.
- Equally, if you're finding it useful, do keep at it for a little longer.

After you've finished:

- You can re-read what you've written if you like – either the next day, before starting the next session, or at the end of the week.
- If you prefer, you can throw the writing away or destroy it: by deleting your file or, if it's on paper, burning it, tearing it up, or throwing it into the sea.
- Review how you feel after you've finished your four days. If you've found it helpful, keep going. It's an easy tool you can use whenever you feel like it.

'Getting stuff onto paper often makes me realise things are not as bad as I thought, and it's good to look back on previous entries which show that I've been in the black treacle before and made it out the other side.' **Andrea**

Writing can be revealing and therapeutic. But what if you've had enough of words, or analysing, or ruminating? Back to Sarah...

Arts and crafts as therapy

I have had a life-long interest in art, both as a practitioner and observer. One of my earliest memories is of drawing at nursery school, inhaling the scent of magic markers, listening to them squeak as I scribbled away and now, half a century later, illustrating this book has given me a similar childlike pleasure. I've noticed that when my brain is tired of writing I still have energy to draw; this may be because it involves different neural pathways.

Touchingly, my father, who suffered from Alzheimer's disease, retained his ability to draw long after his ability to write lengthy prose had gone.

This sort of occupational therapy has been used in the treatment of mental illness for eons; work in the needle room, laundry and kitchen was prescribed to able-bodied female patients of Bethlem (Bedlam) lunatic asylum in the nineteenth century[40]. Soldiers returning from WW1 were taught to stitch as active therapy for 'shell shock'[41] – psychological trauma caused by trench warfare. At about the same time, the great Swiss thinker, Carl Jung[42], convinced that drawing might aid self-exploration, began encouraging his patients to experiment with mandalas – designs which use concentric lines and circles and have their origins in India. These days, seeing an art therapist might involve drawing or making something and talking about yourself and your interrelations, but you don't have to consult a professional to benefit from the healing power of art. As the huge sales of colouring books over recent years testify[43], it's a very accessible form of self-help.

'I like to colour in. As I take a flat page and make it live, I find I lose myself, and only think about the colouring. Each stage of colouring adds more to it. It lets my brain rest and stops the worrying and constant thinking.' **Jan**

'I make cards and cross-stitch bookmarks for a local hospice shop so my creativity helps me and is helping others too.' **Lily**

[40] http://thetimechamber.co.uk/beta/sites/asylums/asylum-history/the-history-of-the-asylum
[41] http://www.thehistoryblog.com/archives/29681
[42] http://networkmagazine.ie/articles/art-therapy-harnessing-healing-potential-creativity
[43] https://www.psychologytoday.com/blog/worry-and-panic/201508/why-colouring-books-are-red-hot-in-self-help-right-now

TRY THIS: Painting pebbles

Pebble painting is an easy activity and can be done indoors or out.

- You will need pebbles, and if you have a design in mind e.g. a cat or owl, look out for the right shape to be your canvas. Smooth, rounded stones make the best surface, so pebbles found on the beach or by a river are often ideal, but please make sure you are allowed to take them[44]. Alternatively, many craft shops sell a selection of pebbles in bags.
- Your paint needs to be waterproof and weather proof. You can either use a mixture of two parts acrylic paint to one part PVA glue, or a chalk-based paint followed by clear varnish.
- Make sure your pebble is clean. Wash it with warm water and soap and pat it dry. You could even scrub it with an old toothbrush. Some stones have rough patches on them that will make painting a little more difficult. You can sand the pebble with sandpaper, starting with a coarse paper and moving to fine one until the rough patch is gone.
- It might be wise to try out your design on paper beforehand. When you put it onto the rock, use a pencil or chalk and be sure not to press too heavily since it can show through the paint. If you're stuck for ideas, here is some inspiration:

- Now you're ready to start painting. Be patient and move from the biggest parts of the design to the smallest, letting each coat dry before moving on – use a hairdryer if need be!
- Once you've finished painting and your pebble is dry, seal it. Two coats of sealant will ensure your art lasts a long time.

Painted pebbles have many uses. You could make them into fridge magnets - use a light pebble and glue a magnet on the back

[44] www.theguardian.com/environment/green-living-blog/2011/jun/29/coastlines-marine-life-beach-forage

when you're finished. Or make paperweights – heavier stones are better for this purpose, decorate your garden, create seasonal decorations or write inspiring messages on them.[45]

Gardening as therapy

Drawing and painting can be enjoyed outdoors, but arguably the best way to be creative in the fresh air is gardening. And you don't need a vast estate to relish it, believe me; my patio is tiny – and *rammed* with flowers. It doesn't matter if you are rich or poor, seven or seventy, plants don't give a fig about who is tending them, and it can boost self-esteem to participate in such a transformative activity.

Cultivating other living things can take us out of ourselves – when we're depressed we often become solipsistic, so it's helpful to be gently reminded we are not the centre of the universe. Yet whilst it shows us we're part of something bigger, **gardening also allows us to feel safe**. To dig and delve in a walled or fenced garden helps to contain us within boundaries both literally and metaphorically, so we feel secure at the same time as expanding our horizons. No wonder we are a nation of gardeners!

Gardening helps us relax and let go, and there's a neurological reason: **working in nature releases happy hormones**. When we exercise, levels of serotonin and dopamine (the hormones that make us feel good) rise and the level of cortisol (the hormone associated with stress), is lowered. It's true that a day in the garden can leave you ready to hit the hay earlier than usual, but it can also get rid of excess energy so you sleep better and wake feeling renewed inside.

In the plant world, regeneration is a matter of course, but psychological repair does not necessarily come so easily to us as human beings. **One way of facilitating the healing process is through rituals, and gardening is a form of ritual**. As such it works within our minds as a symbolic act involving the giving of life, which can lift the spirits when we're down. Yet whilst the rhythm of tasks such as weeding, hoeing, sowing and sweeping means thoughts can ebb and flow along with our movements in a peaceful

[45] This exercise also appears in *More Making Friends with Anxiety* by Sarah Rayner. If you want to explore arts and crafts therapies, it contains many other suggestions too.

fashion, **gardening also allows us to vent aggression**. Anger issues can be linked to depression[46] so it's helpful to find safe ways to let off steam, but why beat pillows with a baseball bat when you have a hedge to hack? The great thing about destructiveness in the garden is that it can be in the service of growth – if you don't cut back plants, you'll be swamped by them.

Perhaps most valuable of all, being amongst plants and flowers reminds us to live in the present moment, and we'll be returning to the topic of living 'in the now' in Chapter 10. Meanwhile, **tending to plants allows us to tap into the carefree part of ourselves** with no deadlines, mortgage or annoying colleagues to worry about. So why not make an appointment with Mother Nature today?

TRY THIS: Being in nature

'God Almighty first planted a garden; and, indeed, it is the purest of human pleasures,' wrote essayist Francis Bacon back in 1625. He has a point: **gardening engages all the senses**. So next time you're in a garden, pause for a few moments and allow yourself to **be aware of what's around you. Inhale. Look. Listen. Touch.** Experiencing the fullness of nature can be very restorative.

Cooking as therapy

Kate says: One of the most creative activities around needs no expensive new equipment, or fancy supplies. And you probably have an entire room in your house dedicated to it already – your kitchen!

'I like to try new recipes when I cook – it helps me feel creative and self-nourishing.' **Ana**

[46] http://www.nhs.uk/conditions/stress-anxiety-depression/pages/about-anger.aspx

If you're responsible for shopping and cooking for your household, it might take a bit of re-framing to see cooking as a creative act. But it really can be therapeutic:

- **Cooking is satisfying and low-risk**: it's a manageable task that produces an outcome you can enjoy.
- **Cooking is inexpensive and familiar**: you have most, if not all, the equipment and ingredients you need.
- **Cooking creates something new** that you can enjoy right now.

Baking can bring particular cheer: it fills the house with sweet aromas, and we often then reach out to share our delicious creations with others. The novelist Marian Keyes writes movingly and wittily of her experiences of depression, in her recipe book, *Saved by Cake*[47]. She took antidepressants, had therapy and treatment in a psychiatric hospital, and felt so desperate that she even planned how she'd commit suicide, if her mood fell even lower. But things changed after she decided to bake a birthday cake for a friend. Marian had never baked before, but the experience transformed her mood. She found the careful weighing and measuring calming, and the creation of cupcakes or scones from raw ingredients was rewarding but not overwhelming.

Another example of cake as therapy comes from the worldwide Depressed Cake Shop movement – it started as a 'pop-up' shop in the UK, where people baked grey 'depressed' cakes, with small glimpses of colour to symbolise hope. The bakers and customers came together to eat, and talk about mental illness in a way that broke down taboos. Find out more or organise your own via their site, http://depressedcakeshop.com.

TRY THIS: Cooking up a treat – three quick mood-boosting recipes

It doesn't *have* to be cake (though if you love baking, Marian's book has some wonderful recipes). It can simply be an old favourite recipe that you find comforting, or an idea you've spotted in a magazine that makes your mouth water. Or try one of the very adaptable recipes I've written below.

As you cook, take note of how you feel before, during and after:

---

[47] Saved by Cake, Marian Keyes, Michael Joseph 2012

- What do you enjoy the most? The planning, preparing – or the eating? You can use this to decide on sessions.
- Photograph ingredients, and the end result – and think about sharing on social media if you like reaching out. People on Facebook, Pinterest and Instagram *love* photos of good food! And it's also a great place to get new ideas.

- Make a ritual out of serving what you've made: as we mentioned in Chapter 3, taking time to enjoy your food, especially when it's home-made, offers a calm, soothing interval in your day.

Below are three part-recipes, part techniques, to be adapted to whatever you have handy or is in the shops. Enjoy adapting them to your own tastes.

Vegetable Soup – the great comforter

Soup is a like a hug in a bowl and so easy. This makes 3-4 portions. Keep covered in the fridge for up to 3 days or freeze in individual portions.

You need:

- **1 saucepan**
- **1 hand blender** if you want to puree the soup
- **1-2 tablespoons fat**: olive oil, rapeseed oil, butter, coconut oil
- **1 onion** (or substitute a stick of celery)
- **Fresh flavourings:** try chopped garlic, a fresh chilli (wash your hands afterwards)

- **Herbs and spices:** Choose your favourites from the spice rack or the garden. Add whole spices and bay leaves/dried herbs/ rosemary or thyme to the cooking pot. Fresh mint, parsley, basil and coriander are best added just before serving or as a garnish.
- **400g vegetables**: use seasonal produce – cheaper and tastier – or frozen veg like peas (delicious with mint) or carrots.
- **75g leaves**: baby spinach, kale, chard, spring greens. Wash well and remove any very thick stems.
- **Store cupboard extras:** a can of chopped Italian tomatoes, or a drained can of cooked lentils or beans adds body and flavour.
- **750ml stock**: use vegetable bouillon powder or chicken stock/cubes.
- **Your choice of toppings:** fresh herbs, grated cheese like cheddar or Parmesan, a spoonful of Greek yogurt or crème fraiche, a sprinkling of seeds, a dash of hot chilli sauce...

Method:

- Chop onion and garlic or chilli if using. Heat the fat in the saucepan and add the onion or celery with any dried herbs or spices or spice pastes and cook gently for 5 minutes till the vegetables are translucent. Meanwhile, chop root veg like potatoes or carrots into cubes, and slice green vegetables.
- Add the vegetables to the pan along with any woody herbs like thyme or rosemary and let them cook – root vegetables benefit from browning a tad. Now add the stock and bring to the boil.
- Let the soup simmer until the toughest vegetables are just soft – for carrots or potatoes, this might take 20-25 minutes, for green beans or cauliflower, much less.
- Add leaves, if using, and let them wilt for 2-3 minutes. Puree the soup using a hand blender if you wish. Season with black pepper and sea salt. Serve with toppings and a chunk of good bread.

My favourite combinations:

- **Carrot and coriander**: 400g carrots, 1 onion, 1 clove garlic, 1 teaspoon ground coriander: to serve, 1 tablespoon of yogurt, with fresh parsley or fresh coriander on the top.
- **Sweet potato and chilli**: 400g sweet potatoes, peeled; 1 red onion, 1 fresh chilli, 1 teaspoon ground cumin or curry

powder/garam masala: to serve, a little chilli sauce and some fresh chives.

- **Cauliflower cheese**: 1 small head of cauliflower divided into florets; 1 onion, 1 small potato, diced: a teaspoon of wholegrain mustard; to serve, grated Cheddar cheese.

A pick-and-mix main course salad

Here's a challenge – how many rainbow colours can you include?

You need:

- **1 main ingredient:** tuna, roast chicken, turkey, smoked salmon, avocado, goat's cheese, feta, halloumi cheese, hummus, falafel
- **Leaves:** little Gem lettuce, rocket and watercress mix, young spinach, shredded red cabbage
- **Grains:** optional, but you can make a salad more filling by adding cooked grains, like bulgar/cracked wheat, farro (Italian emmer wheat), barley, wild rice
- **Vegetables:** cherry tomatoes, spring onions, grated carrot, cooked and diced potato, fresh sweet peppers or roasted peppers from a jar, artichoke hearts, mange tout, baby corn
- **Dressing:** in a bowl or jam jar, combine 3 tablespoons of extra-virgin olive oil (or fancier oils if you have them: avocado, rapeseed, hazelnut or even sesame for an Asian style dressing) with 1 tablespoon vinegar (cider, wine, balsamic rather than malt) or lemon juice. Add a clove of crushed garlic, fresh herbs, salt, pepper or ½ teaspoon French mustard. Shake or mix well.
- **Topping(s):** pitted or stuffed olives; sesame, pumpkin or sunflower seeds; berries like raspberries blueberries or dried goji berries; almonds, cashew nuts, pecans; parmesan or similar cheese shavings (use a potato peeler).

Method:

Arrange on a plate, pour over dressing, add toppings and enjoy!

A fruit salad with extras

Whole fruit salads are colourful, tempting and so much more satisfying than smoothies, so follow this simple plan to create your own. Choose ripe fresh, or frozen fruits: dried fruit is high in sugar so best used as a topping, in small quantities. It's good to add some fat/protein in the form of nuts, dairy or seeds to balance out the dish.

- **Fruits:** choose 3, of different colours. Apples, bananas, berries, (don't dismiss frozen berries – often cheaper and always on hand), fig, grape, kiwi, mango, melon, nectarine, orange, peach, pear, plum, pineapple, and so many more.
- **Dressing**: Depending on the fruit, you may not need to 'dress' the salad. But if you want to, choose 75ml fresh juices like apple, cranberry, orange.
- **Topping:** Greek yogurt, crème fraiche, nuts, seeds, ground nut and flaxseed mixes, a little shaved dark chocolate, dried fruit, granola, pomegranate seeds, passionfruit pulp.

Simply slice or chop your fruits and combine, with dressing if using. Refrigerate if you plan to eat later – add topping just before serving.

Whatever activity you try, remember the process is at least as important as the outcome. Creativity is part of being human – and even a few precious moments absorbed in cooking, gardening, art or writing reminds us there is life after depression.

9. 'O' is for Overcoming Depression

Maybe it's the first morning that you wake up and notice the birdsong and the blue sky instead of a familiar sense of dread. Or it might be the moment after a laughter-filled chat with a friend when he or she says, 'You know, you seem different. More like your old self.' Or perhaps the world simply seems brighter, funnier, more inviting.

Emerging from a depressed state may sometimes feel like 'two steps forward, one back'. But one thing all of us have in common as we begin to feel better is the desire never to return to *that place*. So this chapter is about **taking steps to sustain our recovery** *and* about **building up our reserves and resilience to reduce the chances of a relapse**.

Better – and wiser?

After my first bout of depression, I hoped that was that: no more blues. In fact, I've now realised that I *am* susceptible to relapse. Some people have dodgy knees that plague them through life, or chronic eczema. My weak spot is the blues, and I've learned to live with it.

But learning is key. When I did become depressed a second time, I knew that recovery was possible – even though that light at the end of the tunnel was often barely visible.

In many ways, the options for people with mental health issues have widened since my first bout. Research on positive psychology – the steps we can take to feel good about ourselves and our lives – has blossomed, while the internet has allowed sufferers to share their experiences, and do their own research on approaches that can work.

For me, it's a bit like clearing up after an unexpected hurricane. Imagine a home that's been ravaged by wind, leaving it exposed, perhaps on the point of collapse. The first thing you do is to shore it up, make emergency repairs to keep it functioning,

After the storm passes, you then rebuild, but stronger. You dig deeper foundations, make the walls and windows more weather-proof, look at which of your neighbours did better and learn from them. And you definitely pay closer attention to the weather forecast...

Downtime: The figures on feeling better and relapse

According to NICE, the average length of a depressive episode is 6–8 months[48]. What about relapse? NICE guidelines state that the risk of depression returning is:

- At least 50% after a first episode of depression, 70% after a second episode and 90% after a third episode.
- That risk of recurrence increases in people under 20 years of age, and in older patients.

[48] http://cks.nice.org.uk/depression

As you begin to feel better, it's essential to talk to your doctor before stopping medication, as sudden withdrawal from anti-depressants can lead to relapse, and/or unpleasant side effects. 'Tapering off' the dose, under supervision, is the best way to avoid this[49]. In some cases of depression, it's recommended that medication is continued for up to two years, to reduce the risk of recurrence.

Other techniques like individual CBT and Mindfulness-Based Cognitive Therapy (MBCT) are also recommended by NICE under some circumstances to help prevent relapse[50] – talking to your doctor or mental health professional means you can look at these options together.

Early warnings: Staying alert

If you're feeling better – hurrah – thinking about relapse is probably the last thing you want to do! But being alert to your own behaviours, especially negative changes, means you can monitor how you're doing and seek help sooner, if needed.

These are signs that might suggest a relapse:

Physical changes

- Sleep disruption: continuing insomnia or increased sleepiness.
- Fatigue – finding it harder to get things done – or the flipside, excess energy that we can't burn off whatever we do.
- Weight changes: depression can make us lose our appetite, or comfort eat.
- Increased aches and pains: we may notice pain more, or be less able to cope with it.

Behavioural changes

- Withdrawing from social contact and activities you enjoy.
- Having more arguments or being more irritable.
- Drinking more alcohol, taking more street drugs.

Mental changes

- Low mood – less enjoyment of daily life.

[57] See also page 30 and http://www.mims.co.uk/antidepressants-guide-switching-withdrawing/mentalhealth/article/882430
[50] https://www.nice.org.uk/treatment-choice-based-on-depression-subtypes-and-personal-characteristics#continuation-and-relapse-prevention

- Ruminating or falling back into cycles of negative thinking, such as those we describe in Chapter 4.
- Increased anxiety or overwhelm.

Of course, we all have occasional sleepless nights or days when we want to shut the world out. You won't always want, or need, treatment, even if depression does recur. But if you're noticing symptoms that don't go away, talk to someone: family or friends, or your doctor.

'I do believe you're never a million miles away from depression once you've had it, so it's important to take care and remain aware.' **Jeannette**

TRY THIS: Keep a mood diary

It can take any form – a simple score out of ten for how you feel at the same time each day, notes on any changes you're worried about, or even doodle faces that match your mood. You can also use apps like **moodscope.com** or **moodpanda.com** to monitor feelings. This is a great way to spot patterns, or cause and effect – for example, I definitely feel gloomier just before my period. Sometimes I fear the worst – when I check my calendar and realise I'm pre-menstrual, it's always a big relief. A diary can also help if you want talk to a doctor or someone close to you about concerns that depression might be returning.

Building stronger foundations: Resilience

When we're feeling sunnier, we're in a good place to adopt positive habits and work on our resilience: the ability to cope with unwelcome events that life throws at us.

Resilience is closely connected to self-esteem (see Chapter 5). Resilient people still experience negative responses to difficult circumstances – but they have **good coping strategies that protect them** from being badly affected. Early work on resilience in the 1970s and 1980s looked at how groups of children growing up with alcoholic or schizophrenic parents went on to respond to difficult times. Many exhibited self-destructive traits, but a third were judged as 'resilient' – they found positive ways to respond to negative events.[51]

[51] https://en.wikipedia.org/wiki/Psychological_resilience and Werner, E. E. (1989): Vulnerable but invincible: a longitudinal study of resilient children and youth.

The good news is that we can actively work on building our resilience. It might seem counter-intuitive, but my experiences of depression *have* helped me because I've made a concerted effort to boost my foundations. It's almost like a force-field – bad things may happen, but they bounce off more readily than before.

Many of the tools from Chapters 4 and 5 are effective in building resilience. In addition the American Psychological Association suggests[52]:

- **Building closer connections** with friends, family or the community, by joining groups or volunteering.
- **Tackling problems with decisive action**, rather than hiding from them. There's more on decision-making in Chapter 10.
- **Learning from stressful situations** and recognising that crises don't last forever.
- **Setting achievable goals** – ask 'what's the one thing I could accomplish today that takes me in the right direction?'
- **Nurturing a positive view of yourself** and your problem-solving abilities.

Yale University psychologist, Patricia Linville, also found that **it helps to view ourselves as having different roles or 'layers'**[53]. If we're focused on one thing – like trying to be the perfect parent or boss – then if something goes wrong in that area, we'll tend to be hit harder. It's similar to the strategy mentioned on page 66, where we emphasized the value of having several positive roles or activities. You can increase your 'layers' by looking for new activities you enjoy and forming new social networks.

TRY THIS: Reaching out

Connecting with others doesn't have to be daunting. There are lots of 'quick-wins' you can use to build bridges and increase positive interactions with the world.

---

[52] http://www.apa.org/helpcenter/road-resilience.aspx

[53] Self-complexity as a cognitive buffer against stress-related illness and depression. Linville PW, 1987.

- Chat with people in 'safe' situations – go to a favourite café or shop, and talk to the owner or staff about business, their recipes or latest window display.
- Pay a compliment: finding ways to compliment someone helps us look outwards, rather than inwards. Plus it can make their day!
- Borrow a dog – people really do chat to you more when you have a canine companion. Or simply ask a friendly dog-walker about *their* pooch. It's a safe, easy topic.
- Ask for advice: people love to be asked their advice, it's flattering to be seen as an expert on something.
- Get social online: there's lots of criticism of social media, yet the warmth and advice offered by Facebook groups, for example, has been life-changing for me.
- Or try a visual platform like Instagram or Pinterest to see beautiful, cheering images and share your own.

Treating yourself

We've talked often about being your own best friend, and that shouldn't end just because you might not be depressed anymore. Self-care – eating well, exercising, getting proper rest – is important in avoiding relapse. Remember too that even positive changes, like a new job or a new home, can put us under stress. It's not just about maintaining good routines – it can also be about treating yourself to nice things, as a best friend would. Even better, they don't have to cost a penny.

TRY THIS: 10 minute-mood boosters

These are quick ways to boost your mood and make you feel good about yourself. Think of them as like mini-breaks from your daily life, without the cost of a hotel or a flight...

- **Music therapy:** find your favourite mood-boosting track and play it full blast, dancing around your living room (you may want to close the curtains first). Better still, make an upbeat playlist.

- **Laughter therapy:** laughter yoga is an actual class, but it's cheaper to search on YouTube for your top comedy moments. Chances are, the scenes you love – whether it's Laurel and Hardy, Del Boy and his chandelier, or Frasier's finest moment – will be online. Or find a comedy podcast to listen to as you commute or exercise.
- **Walk this way:** a ten-minute walk outside can pep up your circulation and improve your mood, especially if you can include some greenery as part of the view.
- **Hard labour:** short bursts of physical work can be really energising – whether it's clearing the back garden, or doing a high-speed tidy up of your entire house, you'll feel a great sense of achievement and can reward yourself any way you choose.

Hopefully these ideas have inspired many more of your own. So find or buy a nice notebook and jot down ideas for treats or mood-boosters whenever you think of one. The activities in Chapter 8 are a great starting point. Whenever you're having a stressful day, flick through your Mood Boost Directory and prescribe yourself a treat or two...

<u>Riding the ups and downs</u>

'I definitely have a cycle of 6-9 months going from a wonderful sense of wellbeing to just feeling low. I choose to think positively and I've learnt to recognise and enjoy the high and embrace the low. Neither mood is too excessive, so I look forward to good times.' **Helga**

Depression changes us, whether it returns or not. But part of Making Peace with Depression is recognising that the downs can have their upsides: our sensitivity can make us more empathetic towards other people. Our ability to talk about feelings can improve our relationships. The good habits we adopted to see us through the illness can have positive effects on our wellbeing for the rest of our lives. And what we've learned about ourselves can help us to make changes for the better.

I'm certainly not like the children's book character, Pollyanna, who was so optimistic she was able to play the 'Glad Game' in painful circumstances. But if you've experienced depression, you'll know that life isn't only about finding your way out of the dips: it's also about recognising – and celebrating – the highs. Hold on tight...

10. 'N' is for Next – living in the now

We're nearly at the end of our journey through this book. If you're concerned you won't remember it all, or worried about putting the suggestions into practice, this chapter should help. It is designed as a standalone, recapping what's gone before and finishing with some easy tips, so you can turn straight to it in times of need.

D.E.P.R.E.S.S.I.ON. – a summary of what we've learned

1. Diagnosis can be helpful. Because our understanding of the brain, particularly its higher functions, is not as advanced as many other areas of medicine, **psychiatric diagnosis is not perfect. It can lead to the over-medicalisation of normal experiences and take too little account of variation. Nonetheless it has a crucial role to play in obtaining high-quality, safe care.** Seeing your doctor is a helpful step. If you have problems connecting with one GP, please don't give up. Make an appointment to see another.

2. Expert support will ease your journey to recovery. If you're experiencing a major depressive episode, it's no wiser to try to get through it all alone than it would be to undertake surgery on yourself. You'll experience more pain because you don't have the skills or the perspective to undertake your own treatment, especially if you've not been through depression before. But that doesn't mean relying 100% on your GP. As Patrick admits, being a doctor in a General Practice entails being something of a 'Jack-of-all-trades', with a broad understanding of numerous medical conditions and diseases. GPs also don't have much time. In cases of very severe depression it may be worth seeing a psychiatrist, but in any event, **a good counsellor or therapist can be a huge boon**.

Also, expert care needn't mean handing yourself over to others with complete passivity. There is benefit to educating yourself – **becoming an expert in your own mental health is empowering, and means you can play a big part in your own recovery**. You'd rather try therapy or counselling than medication? It's your body and your mind, so make that clear when you see the professionals, and start there. If, after a few weeks, the route you've chosen is not helping, you can always review the situation. And don't forget to keep talking to your loved ones – friends and family members who maybe keen to help but unsure how. If they're struggling, try telling them what works for you in terms of support. Avoid criticizing them (as this may make them defensive) and focus on the positives.

3. Physical symptoms are common – depression is a 'dis-ease' of the body as well as the mind. It often lowers energy levels, affects appetite, sleep and a whole lot more. **Caring for ourselves physically can be a good way to begin 'making friends' with depression on a day-to-day basis**. Eat well, stay hydrated and endeavour, if possible, to exercise. Whilst it can be tempting to stay

safe indoors snuggled in a blanket, fresh air can clear the head and being in nature can lift the spirits. Anything that requires you to be active is positive – planting primroses, pogo-ing to punk music, playing ping pong, walking the dog – if you've the urge, go for it!

4. Responding negatively to people, circumstances and events can continue the cycle of depression. Thinking how you *should* be behaving, or worrying about what other people think will only make you feel more miserable. **The negative thoughts you are having are similar to those we all have from time to time, just the volume is turned up more loudly on yours, and the aim is to turn that volume down. So see if you can become more aware of ways in which you are especially tough on yourself or inclined to get caught up in worry, and try to stand back a little.** By changing the way you approach your low mood, you can start to manage your own depression, rather than your depression managing you.

5. **Poor self-esteem is associated with low mood as people who lack belief in themselves are more concerned with getting approval from others and tend to be less able to be happy just being themselves**. Learning to say 'no' and developing a clearer sense of your own boundaries – what's OK and what's not OK – can help improve self-confidence, which in turn can help move you further along the mood spectrum and away from feeling extremely blue.

6. **'Safety behaviours'** are familiar but damaging ways we behave such as drinking and eating too much, isolating ourselves and avoiding situations that may trigger us. All these can perpetuate depression, and **as with negative thinking, learning to spot our own coping mechanisms and destructive habits** ***as we are using them*** **is crucial if we're trying to break the hold they have over us**. In the longer term, facing our fears gradually and without props, using the stepping stones approach, can help us reach our goals.

7. **Suffering is part and parcel of depression, and should never be underestimated.** Just because we don't look ill, doesn't mean we aren't in agony. **Please reach out if you feel this low**[54]. Even though things seem hopeless, **there is a going to be a way forward that you haven't considered**. Depression prohibits us from thinking clearly, and someone 'outside' your head has more chance of helping to find a way through than you do.

8. **Imagination** can fuel depression by leading us to believe the very worst about ourselves and others, but it **can also help us heal.** Music, poetry, prose, paintings and sculpture can reach out to us in our in pain, and just as reading, listening and looking at others' work can bring relief and solace, so can being actively creative. Writing, drawing, gardening, cooking, dancing, singing – it doesn't matter which activity you choose – **expressing ourselves creatively can benefit the heart and mind.**

[54] Speak to a friend or relative, or, if you are in danger of self-harming right now, please call an ambulance, go straight to A&E or call the Samaritans for free on 116 123 to talk.

9. Overcoming depression doesn't, unfortunately, mean it's wise to forget about the experience entirely, however strong the urge once you're through the worst. Just as it can be helpful in the long term to learn from relationships that haven't worked out and use that knowledge to figure out who might be better suited to us next time, so it is with depression. If we stick our heads in the sand and ignore the opportunities for learning that depression gives us, chances are we'll fail **build up the reserves and develop the resilience that can reduce the chances of a relapse.** The better we understand and care for ourselves, the greater the likelihood of enjoying prolonged periods of good mental health and happiness.

10. Having gained better understanding of your depression, what next? Rather than focusing on the future, which may trigger anxiety, it seems more helpful to end this book by focusing on the present day – where you are at *now*. In this way you more likely to remain grounded and keep your goals realistic. Over-reaching yourself in the weeks and months following a major depression may mean you fail and come crashing down again. **So** here are six suggestions on how to maintain a more balanced life day-to-day.

A balanced life

1. Express gratitude. We tend to focus more on the bad than the good, especially when we're depressed, and research suggests this is because negative information represents a threat to our survival[55]. Making time to give thanks offsets this bias, and neuroscientist Alex Korb has shown that feeling grateful can benefit the brain. It starts with the dopamine system, because expressing gratitude activates the brain stem region that produces dopamine. It also boosts the neurotransmitter serotonin, just as many antidepressants do.[56]

Here are three ways to practise gratitude:

- **Appreciate happy memories.** Research[57] suggests that spending time reflecting back on positive past experiences or people we have cared for can increase happiness and decrease loneliness.
- **At the end of each day, look for small things to be grateful for.** Have you received a helping hand from a stranger? An invitation you can look forward to? Did someone cook you a nice meal or did you watch your favourite TV series? Life is a series of moments so value the ones that lift your heart, however seemingly inconsequential.
- **Give thanks for having your basic needs met.** People who lack access to necessities know this all too well, but for the rest of us it can be easy to forget how lucky we are, says psychologist Juliana Breines. Every time you have access to clean water, food, a bed, or heat if it's cold, you have something to be thankful for.[58]

2. Make decisions. Kate touched on the value of taking decisive action on page 112, and neuroscience backs up the theory it can help us feel better. As well as helping you solve problems, research shows that making decisions reduces worry and anxiety. **Making decisions includes creating intentions and setting goals** – all three are part of the same neural circuitry and engage the prefrontal cortex in a positive way. Being decisive also helps overcome striatum activity, which usually pulls you toward negative impulses and routines.[59]

---

[56] http://assets.csom.umn.edu/assets/71516.pdf
[57] https://www.ncbi.nlm.nih.gov/pubmed/21787094
[58] https://www.psychologytoday.com/blog/in-love-and-war/201411/10-things-you-can-be-thankful-no-matter-whats-going?collection=152715

TIP: Don't procrastinate. Making decisions can be hard, but trying to be perfect tends to overwhelm us with emotions and make us feel out of control. So make a 'good enough' decision and be kind to your brain. If you *still* find it impossible to decide what to do, break it down into manageable stepping stones.

3. Seek company. Again, Kate touched on this, but don't just take our word for it: neuroscience shows that relationships are important to your mind's feeling of happiness. A recent fMRI[60] experiment demonstrated that social exclusion activates the same brain circuitry - the anterior cingulate and insula - as physical pain[61]. No wonder that loneliness is so distressing, yet when we're depressed it can be very tempting to persuade ourselves *not* to take the risk and put ourselves out there socially.

TIP: Try to be around folk who sustain you, rather than people who undermine you.

Here the phrase 'nothing ventured, nothing gained' is pertinent. We won't know how much better it can make us feel unless we do it. If you're filled with trepidation, I recommend our Facebook group[62] as a good place to start. Even if you're not someone who usually enjoys social networking, you might be pleasantly surprised by how friendly many members are.

---

[60] Functional magnetic resonance imaging.
[62] [61] From *The Upward Spiral* by Alex Korb.
[62] Making Friends with Anxiety & Depression is at www.facebook.com/groups/makingfriendswithanxiety/ and there is also a Facebook page for the book here: https://www.facebook.com/makingfriendswithdepression/

4. Express yourself. 'Better out than in' might be common parlance, but expressing how we feel can still be hard, especially when these feelings are negative. Yet research shows that even talking about emotions that are as dark as 'I want to kill myself' can lessen the hold these thoughts have on us. It's no coincidence that talking is called a cure – once someone says how they are feeling, they've a better chance of discovering other options to self-harm.[63]

Whatever the level of your distress, it's important **to ventilate** your emotions. If you've no one around to speak to, try verbalizing your thoughts out loud.

TIP: When you feel upset, shout into your pillow; go somewhere isolated and scream as loud as you can; if you feel tearful, allow yourself to cry, or try expressive writing, as detailed on page 96.

5. Be kind to yourself. In some ways, keeping your body and mind healthy is not that different to making sure your car is regularly serviced or your computer is backed-up. I'd even go so far as to say that keeping yourself well is as important as other pursuits society often values more highly such as working or looking after others. Moreover, prioritizing your physical and mental wellbeing isn't anything to feel *guilty* about. It takes trust and kindness and courage to make friends with the various difficult and distressing parts of yourself, so be gentle with your psyche.

TIP: Be your own best friend. But remember, you can't pummel your mind and body into submission, just as you can't force anyone to be your friend. Be empathetic, take it slowly, and reward yourself for how far you've come, rather than rebuking yourself for how far you've yet to go.

[63] http://www.samaritans.org/how-we-can-help-you/myths-about-suicide

6. Appreciate the present. Over the last few years the idea of practising *mindfulness* has become so widespread in the context of recovery from chronic anxiety and depression that mere mention of the word may cause you to glaze over and mutter 'not that old chestnut, I had hoped we'd get through this book without too much mention of it'. But allow me to summarise what mindfulness[64] is about, as many depression sufferers (me included) find some form of it helpful.

Mindfulness is the act of focusing on being in the present, and **is simply being really interested in what is actually happening in our bodies and minds from moment to moment.** So being mindful might involve focusing completely on drinking a hot cup of tea, for instance, and taking in its warmth, smell and taste. Or it might involve gardening or cooking – *the important thing is being aware of what you are doing as you are doing it.* The 'TRY THIS' section on pages 58-59 when I invited you to notice your thoughts was, in fact, an exercise in 'being mindful'.

Indeed, the whole of the approach of this book involves being mindful, as **it entails being willing to turn towards our experiences – both good and bad – rather than trying to make them go away as quickly as possible.** When we are curious in this way, we notice that the symptoms of depression are made up of physical sensations – tension, restlessness, tiredness – and that these bodily sensations come and go. Depression also comprises thoughts and feelings and behaviours, as we've been exploring over the last 120-or-so pages. Hopefully by this point you appreciate that these are temporary too and, like the physical symptoms, they come and go.

With this understanding, we can lessen the hold that the negative experiences we associate with depression have on us. If we

[64] Sometimes mindfulness is conflated with meditation, but the two are not identical and you'll find more on the differences here http://www.medicaldaily.com/mindfulness-meditation-differences-377346 Perhaps this last footnote is an appropriate place to confess that I've never found meditating easy – and should you find it hard to sit and 'do nothing' too, perhaps 'active' mindfulness, where you focus on a gentle activity such as gardening or cooking – or even eating(!), may suit you more.

can look at all these responses with curiosity rather than judgement, then we can step out of our old, fear-based, reactive patterns, and step into *being,* and thus having bite-size experiences that we can deal with from moment to moment. **Ultimately, the present is the only time that matters.** The past is gone and we can't change it; the future is yet to happen and most of it we can't influence anyway.

TIP: Aim to practise being in the here and now. Whatever you're doing, notice what's around you. Think of yourself as an animal (which you are, after all). Cats don't worry about the future or past, do they? Nor do cows, or sheep, or pigs... They just are as they are – purry, munchy, baa-y, snuffly – whatever. So wherever you're at in this present moment, use your breath as an anchor to help you tune into a state of awareness and stillness.

Being aware of the preciousness of the present moment enables us to stop struggling and be more accepting of the situation and our whole selves. And so, ultimately, rather than getting clobbered by the scary proverbial 'black dog' of depression, we can make peace with it and welcome this more manageable hound to be our friend. Because whilst he may not always say what we want to hear, he has our best interests at heart whenever he is at our side.

Our thanks to you

Last but not least, Kate, Patrick and I would like to thank you for reading. We hope this little book has helped unravel a complicated subject, and helped to lift your mood. If so, we would appreciate it if you could **leave a review on Amazon.** This will help others find it

and it's useful to hear what readers thought. We also suggest **you keep this book close to hand**, so if you're having a bad day you can reach for it. Don't forget there is the **Making Friends with Anxiety & Depression** support group here: **www.facebook.com/groups/makingfriendswithanxiety/**

Acknowledgements

Thank you to Laura Wilkinson and my mother, Mary Rayner, for help with editing, to Tom Bicât, for listening to how the book read aloud. We'd also like to thank all the people who participated in the *Making Peace with Depression* Survey, whose individual experiences have illuminated this book. If you've any thoughts on how to improve future editions, please get in touch via **sarah-rayner.com**

For times of need – emergency help

Call the Samaritans free on 116 123, www.samaritans.org or email jo@samaritans.org

There's a guide to mental health crisis services in the UK which you can download as a PDF from MIND, available here: http://www.mind.org.uk/information-support/guides-to-support-and-services/crisis-services/#.WBXptvmLRPY

SupportLine Telephone Helpline: 01708 765200 has details of support lines to help those with postnatal depression, Bipolar UK, Childline and more. Email info@supportline.org.uk and http://www.supportline.org.uk/problems/depression.php

For worldwide suicide hotlines please visit http://www.suicide.org/international-suicide-hotlines.html

www.metanoia.org

About the authors

Sarah Rayner is the author of five novels including the international bestseller, *One Moment, One Morning.* She worked for 25 years as an advertising copywriter and used her marketing knowledge to self-publish *Making Friends with Anxiety,* a little book to help ease worry and panic, in 2014. Its success spurred her to write *Making Friends with the Menopause* and *Making Peace with Depression* in collaboration with Kate and Patrick, and there are now several books in the series. Find her on Facebook, Twitter and **www.sarah-rayner.com.**

Kate Harrison is the author of four non-fiction books about health and diet, as well as 12 novels. She worked as an investigative journalist and BBC correspondent and developed a broad knowledge of diet and nutrition when she embarked on intermittent fasting, which led her to writing *The 5:2 Diet Book.* Her 5:2 titles have sold in excess of 400,000 copies in UK & Commonwealth territories, and been translated into 20+ languages. Find her on Facebook, Twitter and **www.kate-harrison.com.**

Patrick Fitzgerald MB.BS MRCGP Diploma in Palliative Medicine is a General Practitioner working in Cheshire. He studied medicine in London and became a GP in 2007. As a GP he sees people suffering with mental health issues on a daily basis, and is keenly aware of the rising numbers of those troubled by depression and anxiety. He is an advocate of patient-centred care, focusing on shared decision-making with patients. He feels the role of the GP is as medical translator and advisor, communicator, and, mostly, listener.

Useful websites

Depression:

Depression – www.depressionalliance.org; www.depressionuk.org
Suicide – metanoia.org; www.samaritans.org
Bipolar disorder – www.bipolaruk.org
Bereavement – www.cruse.org.uk
Northern Ireland Lifeline: www.lifelinehelpline.info, www.aware-ni.org.uk
Wales – www.callhelpfline.org.uk
Scotland – www.breathspacescotland.co.uk
Befriending and support: – www.maytree.org.uk
For young men – 15-35 www.thecalmzone.net
Postnatal depression – www.apni.org
Moodswings – www.moodswings.org.uk
Sad – www.sada.org.uk

Anxiety:

www.anxietyuk.org.uk
www.supportline.org.uk
www.socialanxietysupport.com
PTSD – www.ptsd.org.uk

Counselling:

www.britishpsychotherapyfoundation.org.uk
www.counselling-directory.org.uk

Addiction – www.alcoholics-anonymous.org.uk
Alzheimer's – alzheimers.org.uk
Tourette's – www.tourettes-action.org.uk

Self-harm

www.youngminds.org.uk
www.youngminds.org.uk/news/blog/filter/self-harm
www.harmless.org.uk

General mental health:

www.mhf.org.uk
www.mind.org.uk

www.moodscope.com
www.rcpsych.ac.uk (Royal College of Psychiatrists)
www.rethink.org
www.health-in-mind.org.uk
www.actionforhappiness.org
www.sane.org.uk
www.time-to-change.org.uk

General health:
www.bupa.co.uk
www.childline.org.uk
www.netdoctor.co.uk
www.nhs.uk
www.patient.co.uk

Recommended reading - books

Depression:

Shoot the Damn Dog, a memoir of depression, Sally Brampton

Depression, The curse of the strong, Dr Tim Cantopher

Reasons to Stay Alive, Matt Haig

The Depression Book: depression as an opportunity for spiritual growth Cheri Huber

Upward Spiral: Using Neuroscience to Reverse the Course of Depression, One Small Change at a Time, Alex Korb

Night Falls Fast: Understanding Suicide, Kay Redfield Jamison

The Unquiet Mind, a memoir of moods and madness, Kay Redfield Jamison

Sunbathing in the Rain, a cheerful book about depression, Gwyneth Lewis

Dark Nights of the Soul, Thomas Moore

Anxiety:

The Feeling Good Handbook, David D Burns

Overcoming Social Anxiety & Shyness, Gillian Butler

Overcoming Insomnia and Sleep Problems: A Self-Help Guide Using Cognitive Behavioural Techniques, Colin A. Espie

Anxiety: Panicking about Panic: A powerful, self-help guide for those suffering from an Anxiety or Panic Disorder, Joshua Fletcher

Feel The Fear And Do It Anyway: How to Turn Your Fear and Indecision into Confidence and Action, Susan Jeffers

My Age of Anxiety, Scott Stossel

Bereavement:

Grief: On Grief and Grieving: Finding the Meaning of Grief Through the Five Stages of Loss, Elisabeth Kubler-Ross David Kessler

Mindfulness and CBT:

Mind Over Mood: Change How You Feel By Changing the Way You Think, Beck, Greenberger and Padesky

Full Catastrophe Living, how to cope with stress, pain and illness using mindfulness meditation, Jon Kabat-Zinn

Sane New World: Taming the Mind, Ruby Wax

Mindfulness, A practical guide for finding peace in a frantic world, Mark Williams and Danny Penman

The Mindful Way Through Depression, freeing yourself from chronic unhappiness Mark Williams, John Teasdale, Zindel Segal and Jon Kabat-Zinn

Dementia and Alzheimer's Disease:

The Forgetting David Shenk

General Mental Health:

What's Normal Anyway? Celebrities own stories of Mental Illness, Anna Gekoski and Steve Broome

The Examined Life, how we lose and find ourselves, Stephen Grosz

The Courage to Create, Rollo May

Recommended reading - articles

Depression:

http://www.helpguide.org/articles/suicide-prevention/suicide-prevention-helping-someone-who-is-suicidal.htm http://www.nytimes.com/2014/08/16/opinion/depression-can-be-treated-but-it-takes-competence.html

http://www.theguardian.com/commentisfree/2014/aug/20/men-suffer-depression-anxiety

http://www.huffingtonpost.co.uk/jamie-flexman/depression-mental-illness_b_3931629.html

https://www.theguardian.com/books/booksblog/2016/oct/10/poet-melissa-lee-houghton-writing-world-mental-health-day

Mindfulness:

http://www.theguardian.com/lifeandstyle/2014/jan/11/julie-myerson-mindfulness-based-cognitive-therapy

http://www.psychologytoday.com/blog/urban-mindfulness/201106/mindfulness-and-anxiety-interview-dr-lizabeth-roemer

https://www.ted.com/talks/judson_brewer_a_simple_way_to_break_a_bad_habit?utm_source=tedcomshare&utm_medium=email&utm_campaign=tedspread

Anxiety:

http://www.newstatesman.com/2014/04/anxiety-nation-why-are-so-many-us-so-ill-ease

http://www.telegraph.co.uk/health/wellbeing/11046587/How-to-detox-your-life-beat-anxiety-through-meditation.html

http://www.theguardian.com/society/2013/sep/15/anxiety-epidemic-gripping-britain

http://www.dailymail.co.uk/health/article-32984/How-treat-anxiety.html

http://www.dailymail.co.uk/femail/article-2614530/The-midlife-crisis-anxiety-epidemic-Palpitations-constant-fear-crippling-panic-attacks-chronic-anxiety-wrecking-lives-generation-women-live-for.html**Panic attacks:**

http://www.dailymail.co.uk/health/article-2156928/How-control-panic-attacks.html

http://www.huffingtonpost.com/julie-sacks/personal-health-_b_5673365.html

THE 'MAKING FRIENDS' SERIES

Making Friends with Anxiety: A warm, supportive little book to help ease worry and panic

Drawing on her experience of **anxiety disorder and recovery**, Sarah Rayner explores this common and often distressing condition with candour and humour. She reveals **the seven elements that commonly contribute to anxiety** including adrenaline, negative thinking and fear of the future and explains why it becomes a problem for many of us.

Packed with tips and exercises and offset by photos and anecdotes from Sarah's life, this companion to mental good health reads like a chat with a friend. If you suffer from panic attacks, a debilitating disorder or simply want to reduce worrying, *Making Friends with Anxiety* will give you a greater understanding of how your mind and body work together, helping restore confidence and control.

More Making Friends with Anxiety: A little book of creative activities to help reduce stress and worry

In *More Making Friends with Anxiety*, Sarah explores the importance of 'making friends with anxiety' in greater depth, and explains how **gentle creative activity can help**. It's packed with **easy, practical things to make and do** which will occupy your hands and calm your mind: * Paint Pebbles * Decorate glass * Make a Collage * Sew a Simple Cover * Bake a Crumble * Carve Wood * Plant a Windowbox * Make a Necklace * Look at Art * Listen to Music … and more.

Written with Sarah's trademark warmth and humour, *More Making Friends with Anxiety* is filled with an array of cheap and easy activities that will inspire and uplift you, nurturing mindfulness and positivity.

Making Friends with your Fertility: a clear and comforting guide to reproductive health

From fertility counsellor Tracey Sainsbury and bestselling author Sarah Rayner comes a full and frank guide. The onset of periods and puberty, egg and sperm production and preparing to conceive naturally, IVF and assisted conception – Tracey and Sarah tackle them all with warmth and humour. Together they take you on a journey not just exploring what happens when things go well (through intercourse, orgasm and pregnancy), but also looking at situations where conception is not so straightforward, as it isn't for the 1 in 6 heterosexual couples experiencing infertility or for those who are single or in same sex relationships and keen to have a baby. There is clear, concise advice on treatment options such as timed sexual intercourse, IUI and ICSI as well as tips on self-nurturing using alternative therapies, plus guidance on alternate pathways to parenthood such as adoption, fostering and surrogacy.

Making Friends with the Menopause: A clear and comforting guide to support you as your body changes

Many women consider the menopause anything but a friend, but together with Dr Patrick Fitzgerald, Sarah Rayner explains why rather than fighting or ignoring the changes our bodies go through, understanding the experience can help us feel a whole heap better.

Just why does stopping menstruating cause such profound hormonal shifts in the body, leading us to react in myriad ways physically and mentally? Here you'll find the answers, along with practical advice on hot flushes and night sweats, anxiety and mood swings, muscular aches and loss of libido, early-onset menopause, hysterectomy and more, plus a simple overview of each stage of the process so you'll know what to expect in the years before, during and after.

Making Peace with Divorce: a warm, supportive guide to separating and starting anew

After 20 years of marriage and three children, full-time mum Pia Pasternack came home one day to find a note on the doormat and her husband gone… Heartbroken, this was the first of a series of revelations that left her and her family reeling. But gradually Pia built herself back up, and together with Sarah Rayner, in this book Pia passes on the lessons she has learned about the legal, financial and emotional implications of separation. Together they guide you through the minefield that accompanies the bust-up of many long-term relationships, exploring sensitive issues such as whether to separate, how to break the news to children (if you have them) and how best to communicate with your ex. You'll find clear and concise guidance on finding a lawyer, filling in forms and reaching a settlement, quick tips and pointers on how to move on.

Making Peace with the End of Life: a clear and comforting guide to help you live well to the last

From GP and hospice doctor Patrick Fitzgerald and bestselling author Sarah Rayner comes a warm and wise companion to help support you and those caring for you in the last months, weeks and days of life.

From the shock of diagnosis, through treatment options and symptom control to the process of dying itself, *Making Peace with the End of Life* tackles these sensitive issues with compassion and honesty. Full of practical advice and important contact information, it will also help to demystify how the NHS and Social Services work, so you can access the best support more easily. And, drawing on Patrick's extensive clinical experience, it also looks at how communicating your wishes to those involved in your care can give a feeling of safety and control over whatever happens in the future.

BESTSELLING FICTION BY SARAH RAYNER

One Moment, One Morning

'Delicious, big hearted, utterly addictive, irresistible' **Marie Claire**

'A real page-turner... You'll want to inhale it in one breath' **Easy Living**

The Brighton to London line. The 07:44 train. Carriages packed with commuters. A woman applies her make-up. Another observes the people around her. A husband and wife share an affectionate gesture. Further along, a woman flicks through a glossy magazine. Then, abruptly, everything changes: a man has a heart attack, and can't be resuscitated; the train is stopped, an ambulance called. For three passengers on the 07:44, life will never be the same again...

The Two Week Wait

'Carefully crafted and empathetic' **Sunday Times**

'Explores an emotive subject with great sensitivity' **Sunday Express**

After a health scare, Brighton-based Lou learns that her time to have a baby is running out. She can't imagine a future without children, but her partner doesn't feel the same way. Meanwhile, up in Yorkshire, Cath is longing to start a family with her husband, Rich. No one would be happier to have a child than Rich, but Cath is infertile. Could these two women help each other out?

Another Night, Another Day

'An irresistible novel about friendship, family and life's blows' **Woman & Home**

Three people, each crying out for help. There's Karen, worried about her dying father; Abby, whose son has autism and needs constant care; and Michael, a family man on the verge of bankruptcy. As each sinks under the strain, they're brought together at Moreland's Clinic. Here, behind closed doors, they reveal their deepest secrets, confront and console one another and share plenty of laughs. But how will they cope when a new crisis strikes?

THE 5:2 DIET BOOKS BY KATE HARRISON

Kate's first book on intermittent fasting includes her own brutally honest diary of weight loss - plus tips, meal suggestions and the fascinating science behind the 5:2 approach.

In her two recipe books, **The Ultimate 5:2 Recipe Book,** and **5:2 Good Food Kitchen,** Kate offers delicious, simple meal ideas for good health, all calorie-counted. She also shares the stories of people whose lives have been transformed by the approach.

5:2 Your Life

5:2 Your Life: Get Happy, Get Healthy, Get Slim shows how you can use the 5:2 approach - making small changes on just two days a week – to transform your love life, family time, career and fitness too. Each week, a new themed set of exercises will help you take control of the things that matter most to you - plus there's a six week meal plan with brand new recipes. Kate looks closely at the evidence behind every task or idea, and her realistic, humorous approach cuts through the usual self-help jargon.

ALL BOOKS OUT NOW in paperback and ebook

29214764R00079

Printed in Great Britain
by Amazon